What others are saying

"Generosity is how God gets ̲̲̲̲̲̲̲̲̲̲̲ words speak volumes about ̲̲̲̲̲̲̲̲̲̲ not only the kind that is faith-first, but also ̲̲̲̲̲̲̲ with personal anecdotes, cutting-edge research, and Scripture that points to the Spirit behind it all, Randy has provided a roadmap into the future for individuals and organizations alike. Indeed, this is a man who has moved others a little bit closer to the Grace of God, and generosity paves the way.

Laurie Beth Jones
Best-selling author of Jesus, CEO*;* The Path*; and* Jesus, Life Coach

Working closely with Randy has allowed me the opportunity of watching him live the principles of generosity with passion, energy, and authenticity. Now, in his new book, Randy invites us and challenges us to discover the tremendous satisfaction and empowerment of living a Christ-like generous life.

Phil Stolberg
Executive VP/General Manager, Brewer Direct

Randy demonstrates what he writes. He has experienced the generous love of God and he deeply reflects that. God is love. God gives. We receive. We too are called to be givers. If you want to understand the benefits and breakthrough of living generously, I recommend this book!

Pat Dirkse
Founder and Pastor of City Church Compton, an Urban Christian Missional Community

I have too much stuff. Randy's words remind me that God created us to be generous. Selfishness leads to despair, while generosity leads to a life filled with meaning, joy, and happiness. I realize I have more than enough. After all, it all belongs to God. I want to learn to give the rest away and live a life of generosity.

Dan Blomberg
Certified Public Accountant

In *Releasing Generosity*, Randy offers insight into how to practice generosity in our daily lives. I can think of no one better to write a book on generosity. I worked with Randy to transition the ownership of the company he founded, Brewer Direct, to his employees through an employee stock ownership plan (ESOP). While Randy could have sold his company for more to an outside third party, he generously rewarded his employees with this gift—which has changed the lives of the employees. As Randy noted in his book, he "gave one gift and now it's multiplying. It released potential."

Aaron Juckett
President and Founder of ESOP Partners LLC

To live generously, you don't need to wait until you have many things in life. Just start with what you have. Each of us can give a smile. Learn to give that to the people we meet every day. By doing that, you are unconsciously moving towards embracing a generous attitude. Though our actions may seem small, if we surrender them into God's hand, they will yield big results.

One day, Jesus taught, "The kingdom of heaven is like a mustard seed, which a man took and planted in his field. Though it is the smallest of all seeds, yet when it grows, it is the largest of garden plants and becomes a tree, so that the birds come and perch in its branches." (Matt. 13: 31-32). The mustard seed is small. But from this seed comes a plant so big, even the birds build nests in it.

Randy is not just the author of this book on releasing generosity, he releases generosity! This book is a gift from Heaven.

Rev. Jimmy Oentoro
Founder / Chairman International Full Gospel Fellowship & World Harvest

RELEASING *generosity*

RELEASING
generosity

WHAT WILL YOU DO
WITH THE LOVE
YOU'VE BEEN GIVEN?

RANDY BREWER

Big Snowy
MEDIA

Releasing Generosity: What Will You Do with the Love You've Been Given?

Copyright © 2019 by Randy Wayne Brewer
All rights reserved.

. . . .

Library of Congress Cataloging-in-Publication Data
Brewer, Randy Wayne, 1961—
Releasing Generosity: What Will You Do with the Love You've Been Given?
Big Snowy Media
1. Religion
2. Spirituality

ISBN 978-0-578-50288-5

Printed in the United States of America

10 9 8 7 6 5 4 3 2 1

This book is dedicated to . . .

My dad who taught me the value of generosity.

*My team at Brewer Direct for joining me
in releasing generosity.*

*All my faith-first clients and causes who
are making an eternal difference in the Kingdom.*

CONTENTS

ACKNOWLEDGEMENTS

Very special thanks to the students of ByGrace Children's Home, Nairobi, Kenya; plus Anointed Crushers and the students supported through World Harvest in Uganda and Indonesia. I am encouraged by your faith, determination, and joy amidst many "third-world" challenges.

Thanks to the "millennials" of International Full Gospel Fellowship, Los Angeles, for accepting this old dude and challenging me to dig deeper. And thanks to my "mature" Care Group for your prayers, friendship, and support.

I am grateful to Jeudy, Shea and Tobias Mom, Jeff and Miriam Riley, Rea Barnes, Eric and Michiyo and Zack, Lyna and Zyriah Thoeun plus Phil Stolberg and Shellie Speer.

Thank you Dave Goetz and Melissa Parks from CZ Strategy for generously helping to put words around my many thoughts.

I love music. God speaks to me though music. Shout out to Hillsong, Bethel, and Elevation Worship. Plus these artists: Carrollton, Newsboys, Daughtry, Stryper, Lincoln Brewster, Anointed Crushers, and Tauren Wells among others.

May you experience the generosity of God as shared in the grace and mercy of Jesus.

I t is my sincere privilege to provide this foreword to *Releasing Generosity*. I say I am privileged, but perhaps I should say "humbled." Why? You will understand in the pages that follow. There are many blessings that await you. As a foretaste, here are three.

This is a deeply personal testimony. Randy invites us to experience with him the rare mixture of his battle with cancer and his continuing discovery of freedom and contentment that comes from the outflow of generosity.

Second, this is a compelling case for God's intent that his people know the blessings and benefits of the purifying flow of generosity in our lives. Randy unpacks scientific research that supports the biblical message that giving produces a joy found nowhere else.

Finally, this book is a heartfelt plea and challenge that we live our lives in such an open-handed way that we breathe life into a world on life-support. Randy challenges us to have no regrets, to be prepared to leave this life "old, broke and exhausted." To use Paul's words, to be "poured out like a drink offering …"

Read this book with an open heart and soft spirit, and

it will reshape your understanding of what it means to live with joyful surrender. Hear Randy's admonition, "Generosity ultimately is about love. We are what we love, and our habits both follow and form our hearts. I love giving and giving is continuing to transform me."

If you let it, Randy's winsome and compelling work will do the same for you.

R. Scott Rodin
Author of more than a dozen books on stewardship and leadership, including The Steward Leader, The Third Conversion, *and* The Sower

I'm the "Fundraising Guy."

So four years ago, when our church planned a four-week series on giving, I wasn't surprised when they asked me to speak on the topic. As the founder of Brewer Direct, an organization that helps raise money for nonprofit organizations, I've spent decades motivating people to give. I've seen people give richly. I've seen lives changed as a result.

If you had asked me what the Bible said about giving, though, I could have recited a handful of verses, like "God loves a cheerful giver" and "Give and you will receive." Personally, I've always enjoyed giving. As a child I was eager to drop my quarter into the offering plate. As my wealth increased, I had an increased desire to give.

But writing a sermon series has a way of pointing out what you don't know that you thought you did. As I dug into my sermon preparation, specifically 2 Corinthians 9, I was struck by a new concept: generosity isn't the same as giving. Generosity is about the love you release from your heart. Paul tells the story of the Macedonians, who, in the midst of extreme poverty, welled up in rich generosity. They weren't praised for the amount they gave but for the heart with which they gave it. They experienced the love of Christ, and that love spilled out.

Giving, I realized, is a result of generosity. It's an overflow of God's love.

As I spoke and wrote on the topic over the course of the next few years, I began to develop a theology of generosity: We were made in God's image, whose very nature is generous, therefore we were made to be generous. That's when I began to wonder, *If we were designed to be generous, then what are we missing when we aren't?* Or framed positively, *What do we gain from being generous?*

I started paying attention to news stories and studies that confirmed what I thought deep down: that generosity benefits the giver. The more you release, the more you get—physically, emotionally, and financially. Repeatedly, I was struck by the realization that we're not able to release, because we aren't first in a position to receive. And in the not receiving, we are not fully living.

For a time, I watched the TV show "Hoarders," thinking about the metaphoric implications. Unable to stuff anything more in his or her home, the hoarder is in no way capable of receiving. It's only when the home is cleaned out that someone can receive the blessing and do the opposite of hoarding: release. Similarly, as Americans, especially, we hold tightly to our finances because we find security in it. But in the hoarding, we fail to receive. Releasing and receiving—they're intertwined. I wondered if this was so in the physical realm as well. Are generous people less worried, less anxious, and less stressed when they hold onto things loosely?

Even while discovering these truths and writing this book, I've wrestled with the metastatic cancer noted from my first book, growing ever so slowly in my lungs. Now, I believe in a God who heals. My God is able and willing. But if my healing doesn't come on this side of heaven this message feels even more important. It's my sincere hope and desire for the message of generosity to unleash more generosity. I want you to understand how you were created. I want to help you to release the love you've been given. In doing so, the flow will touch others and return to you in many forms of blessing.

If I could ask anything as you read this book, it would be this: pray that you would start to see the world through the eyes of the Father. As you do, start today by maybe taking a small step to listen to someone, volunteer your time for a couple hours, or give out of your abundance. Start releasing generosity. Let the love you've experienced overflow into the hearts and lives of others.

We love because he first loved us.

1 JOHN 4:19

As we
release what God has given us,
we release the walking and jumping
and praising God in others.
And in so doing, our generosity
comes back to us in the form of
an abundant life, one filled with
meaning, joy, and a deeper
happiness that only God can give.

CHAPTER 1

LIFE WITH NO OUTLET

I can still remember the first time my father handed me a quarter. I was six years old, and the money came with very little instruction. I could use the quarter for any-thing—gumballs, a toy at the local corner store, or even for savings. My father did say that he thought I would be better served by putting the quarter in the offering plate. Although my dad had given it to me as we left the car for Sunday school class, I was given a real choice: spend it on myself or give it away.

At six years old, I chose to put the quarter in the offer-ing plate at church. I received no "Atta boy" or pat on the head. There was no external validation. The decision was mine. For whatever reason, I felt compelled to be gener-ous, which has become a part of a much larger narrative of my life. I've given the productive years of my life to helping organizations tap into the generosity of their constituents. A focus of the marketing agency that I founded strengthens and supports the fundraising efforts of nonprofits that work with the poorest of the poor, America's homeless. Through the years of helping others raise money, I have encountered thousands of generous people. I have also witnessed on many occasions the difficulty that people face in giving away their wealth as well as their time and talent.

> *I felt compelled to be generous,*
> *which has become a part of*
> *a much larger narrative of my life.*

For some, generosity seems second nature; for others, it's extremely hard to let go of what they've been given. A few of us may be naturally generous with our time and money, but for most, generosity is learned. In this first chapter, I want us to wrestle with how difficult it really is to live a life of generosity, even, or especially, in the developed world where we want for little. Generosity, ultimately, comes down to this question: What will we do with the amazing love that has been given to us? Generosity began at the cross when God first loved us. For God so loved…he gave (John 3:16). When we experience God's love and decide to share it through our time, talent and treasure, we release generosity into the world. It truly is transformational not only for those who receive our gifts but for us as well.

The Difference an Outlet Makes

In Israel lie two larger bodies of water—the Sea of Galilee

and the Dead Sea—with two completely different stories. The Sea of Galilee is a fresh-water lake fed from rain run-off from the mountains of Galilee and the Golan Heights. Familiar to readers of Scripture, the lake sits 695 feet below sea level and is five miles wide and thirteen miles long. The primary water source for all of Israel, the lake is filled by the Jordan River, which also flows out of the Sea of Galilee and eventually into the Dead Sea. The Sea of Galilee has both and inlet and an outlet.

In stark contrast, the Dead Sea has only the Jordan River flowing into it. And no outlet. Much larger than the Sea of Galilee, it is 48 miles long and reaches a depth of more than a thousand feet. The Dead Sea is the lowest place on the surface of the earth at 1300 feet below sea level. It's "dead" because the water is so salty, the direct result of having no outlet. The Sea of Galilee, with both an inlet and an

Generosity, ultimately, comes down to this question: What will we do with the amazing love that has been given to us?

outlet, receives water and gives water. The Dead Sea, however, only receives and never gives.

The two bodies of water illustrate two kinds of people: those who live a life of generosity, and those who do not. Someone who does not have a lifestyle of generosity has no outlet; his or her life is different in kind than someone who has both an inlet and an outlet. While America has been named the world's most generous nation, its citizens celebrated as giving the most to charity, many in the United States struggle with even a modicum of generosity.[1] One study showed that only about three percent of adult Americans give away ten percent (or more) of their income.[2] And about six out of seven Americans give less than two percent of their income while nearly half (44.8%) admit to giving away not even a single dollar.[3] Our nation is much less characteristic of the Sea of Galilee than we might like to believe. In many ways, we are the Dead Sea.

People of faith don't necessarily give more either. In the book, *Passing the Plate: Why American Christians Don't Give Away More Money*, the authors demonstrate that few American Christians donate generously to religious and charitable causes. One of five self-identified Christians gives nothing at all.[4] Generosity is not an inevitable effect of someone coming to faith. It's hard to know, really, what

> *Generosity is not an inevitable effect of someone coming to faith.*

keeps us from giving from our fullness, from lavishing upon others what we've so abundantly been given by God.

Certainly the fear of not having enough always works the edges of our conscious mind. For many who experienced the effects of the Great Recession, especially for those who lost a house or a business, the fear is real. Economists from Texas A&M explored the recession's impact on generosity. It's not surprising that there was a decline in giving during the Great Recession. It might come as a surprise, though, to find that 10 years following the Great Recession, Americans continued to give less. According to the authors of the study, "We found sharp declines in overall donative behavior that is not accounted for by shocks

It's hard to know, really, what keeps us from giving from our fullness, from lavishing upon others what we've so abundantly been given by God.

to income or wealth. These results suggest that overall attitudes towards giving changed over this time period."[5]

It's not so much greed as it is the fear of survival: "Will there be enough for me and my family now and if another recession hits?" The fear of survival can cause us to batten down the hatches. Our world becomes smaller and smaller. Some of it may be situational, but for others there may be a generalized fear about the future that paralyzes us, preventing us from giving either our time or money.

For others, generosity may simply not be on their radars. There's a lack of awareness about the great needs of the world or at least about the disparity between what we have and that of our neighbors. Some might call it indifference, which, according to Nobel Laureate Elie Wiesel, is the opposite of love.[6] Perhaps Americans' lack of generosity is tied somehow to our egos; we're simply too focused on ourselves or the future of our children to think of others. For some, generosity was never modeled or taught. I think it's also possible to be taught generosity and have it modeled for you, but the spirit of generosity simply never takes root. The seed is there but is never watered.

It's not that someone who is ungenerous doesn't necessarily love God or others. Plenty of folks love their church, their pastor, and the ministries that serve them. In a sense, though, these folks take advantage of the church; they are takers, even if unwittingly so. They may

Scripture seems to indicate that wealth may actually make generosity more difficult.

live paycheck to paycheck and simply don't feel they can write a $20, $200, or $2000 check without risking their ability to make their rent or house payment. They have an inlet (the good gifts of God) but no outlet (generosity that flows towards others).

The Camel Problem
Whatever the reasons for an outlet-impaired life, Scripture seems to indicate that wealth may actually make generosity more difficult. In Mark 12:41-42, the writer says Jesus watched as the rich put large sums of money into the temple treasury while a widow gave two small coins which equaled the smallest Roman coin, a copper quadrans. The rich tossed in large sums into the receptacle but retained their fortunes. The widow "put in everything—all she had to live on" (Mark 12:42). Her gift was truly sacrificial; the

rich had not begun to give to her level of sacrifice. The ratio of the amount of her gift relative to what she possessed was off the charts. I cannot relate to the sacrifice of the widow. I have never been poor or given at her level. Her gift exposed her life to greater risk. I have no experience of giving when my very survival appears to be in question. At six years old, I gave pretty much everything I had by putting the quarter in the offering plate, but I didn't fear for my life or where I would sleep that night.

The New Testament examples of people who allowed their resources to master them are many. Jesus provoked his disciples when he told them that it's harder for a camel to pass through the eye of a needle than it is for a rich man to enter the kingdom. The rich young ruler walked away when told he had to give it all way to enter the kingdom of God. It seems as if the more money or time that you have, the more difficult it may be to live a life of generosity. When you have resources, you tend to think you can rely on those resources: "I'll just buy my way out of this situation." It's easy to forget that all gifts come from God when there is no fear about making next month's mortgage payment. And often, among those who carefully build wealth through a life of savings, entrepreneurial efforts, and hard work, there lies a deep fear of losing it all—perhaps because they know how hard it was to create.

A *New York Times* article, "I'm Rich and That Makes Me Anxious," tells the story of Thomas Gallagher. At age 17, he began to deposit $10 a week in a bank account while working as a clerk on the floor of the New York Stock Exchange.

Through the years, he worked his way up to vice chairman of Canadian Imperial Bank of Commerce World Markets and became a member of the Tiger 21 club, a network of individuals that manages over $50 billion worth of investible assets. Among the wealthiest of the wealthiest, Gallagher still worries about his wealth. He writes:

"I still feel, to some extent, that I don't have enough money. Emotionally, I don't come from money; I got very lucky on Wall Street. I've been dealing with a myriad of psychological issues since I retired. I have more money than I had ever imagined, but I still worry—do I have enough, if I live longer than I thought?"[7]

...other kinds of grief can accompany the love of money, including a fundamental discontent and restlessness with life itself.

The "Do I have enough?" mindset is one possible reason wealthy people have been found to be less generous than the poor. Paul Piff, a psychology researcher from University of California recruited a test sample to fill out an online questionnaire that asked them to identify their socio-economic status. In the lab, they were then asked to play a game in which they were given ten credits, which would be cashed out at the end of the experiment. They were then asked if they would like to give away any of those credits to an anonymous partner. The study found that people who had more, or who identified themselves as having more, tended to give less to a stranger.[8]

Generosity is first and foremost a posture, a way of being in the world that says, essentially, "I will not hold tightly to the things I have. My 'stuff' is not significant." The Bible declares that we can't serve both God and money. We love one at the expense of the other. Scripture also says that the love of money is the root of all kinds of evil (1 Timothy 6:10). Let's be clear: it's the love of money (and not money itself) that is the root of all evil. We understand that nuance. And yet it's the second half of 1 Timothy 6:10 that may reveal what's happening to us: "Some people, eager for money, have wandered away from the faith and pierced themselves with many griefs."

Certainly, debt is one grief that pierces the American dream. Most Americans live on the edge financially. Seventy-eight percent of full-time workers said they live paycheck to paycheck, according to a report from Career-Builder.[9] Another study revealed that Millennials (born between 1997 and 2012) have more than $4,000 in credit card debt and another $23,000 in non-mortgage-related debt.[10] The numbers are staggering. Many truly have pierced themselves with many griefs.

In addition to debt, other kinds of grief can accompany the love of money, including a fundamental discontent and restlessness with life itself. More income or accumulation of wealth rarely equals an easier life or more happiness. More money often creates more choices and thus more complexity in our lives. When there are too many choices, instead of freeing us to be happier, we become overwhelmed by our options.[11]

Study after study shows the real limits of wealth and happiness. Once workers hit an annual salary of $105,000, one study found they experienced "reduced life satisfaction and a lower level of well-being."[12] At some point, more is less, not more. Another study found that high income can buy greater life satisfaction but not necessarily more happiness. More money, or a higher income, can create sense of isolation: "Psychologically, the acquisition of wealth—and more generally, possessions that signal high status—makes us want to distance ourselves from others."[13] Such distance can remove us from the suffering of others and caring for them compassionately with the love of God.

More money doesn't equal bigger hearts of generosity. Another study showed that the percentage of income that is given away actually drops the higher the category of income.[14] A friend lives in a community with professionals from the financial services industry. Many of the nonprofits in the community seek to recruit financial services professionals to their boards, thinking that their higher incomes will increase their donations. That makes perfect sense on the face of it, but the truth is that many of the professionals live beyond their means. They live paycheck to paycheck, as I referenced earlier, just like other Americans. While they may want to be more generous, their lifestyle prevents them from doing so.

There seems to be a pattern that the wealthier we

become, the less we tend to care about others or behave in an ethical manner. The best-known study in this branch of research, titled "Higher Social Class Predicts Increased Unethical Behavior," was published in 2012. It found that the higher a subject's self-described social rank, the more candy they took from a jar labeled as being for children.[15] Studies also show that when people acquired power (which is often tied to wealth), they "acted as if they had suffered a traumatic brain injury—becoming more impulsive, less risk-aware, and, crucially, less adept at seeing things from other people's point of view."[16] Those in power often struggle to empathize or sympathize with others. I am not saying categorically that wealthy people are not generous or that they have no compassion. Far from it. Many high-net-worth families are extremely generous with both time and money. I've seen many organizations thrive because of the generosity of major donors. This is not a dig against the super wealthy.

My point is that more money does not automatically equate to more generosity, to a bigger heart, a larger outlet. And often we deceive ourselves in thinking that "when I get more money, I'll give more." The reality is that as we accumulate wealth, we may cling even more tightly to what we have.

The Lakers Truly Matter

I had just completed writing a blog post for our clients at Brewer Direct. The post was about the healing of a lame man. Peter and John were headed to the temple to pray at

3 p.m., like they did many days. Daily prayer was likely part of their ritual. The passage reads:

> One day Peter and John were going up to the temple at the time of prayer—at three in the afternoon. Now a man who was lame from birth was being carried to the temple gate called Beautiful, where he was put every day to beg from those going into the temple courts. When he saw Peter and John about to enter, he asked them for money. Peter looked straight at him, as did John. Then Peter said, 'Look at us!' So the man gave them his attention, expecting to get something from them (Acts 3:1-5).

It is likely that Peter and John had encountered the lame man before. But this time, verse four says they looked straight at him and Peter said, 'Look at us!' While making their way to the prayer service, doing what was right, they stopped this time and offered healing in the name of Jesus. They stopped. And saw. Then Scripture says, "Taking him by the right hand, he helped him up, and instantly the man's feet and ankles became strong. He jumped to his feet and began to walk. Then he went with them into the temple courts, walking and jumping, and praising God" (Acts 3:7-9). It's not just that Peter and John stopped and saw this man—they helped him.

Having completed what I thought was an insightful short article on this passage, I felt proud when I left work that day. As I walked to my car from my office I passed a man in a wheelchair. I wanted to brush past him. I was in a rush to get home.

"Nice Lakers shirt," he said.

"Thanks," I said. I kept walking, and he wheeled up beside me. I stopped for a minute as he began talking about LeBron James and the prospects for the upcoming season. I was anxious to keep moving, but in a few short moments, he let me know that he was excited about his move to an independent living facility. I said goodbye and quickly jumped into my car. And then it hit me: *You idiot! Are you really too busy for a simple conversation?*

...our generosity comes back to us in the form of an abundant life, one filled with meaning, joy, and a deeper happiness that only God can give.

While I didn't completely ignore him, my response was pathetic. I was largely indifferent. So many times, I pass by someone in obvious need. In my better moments, I utter a quick prayer: "Lord help this person," as I rush past. But what if I was supposed to stop and—like Peter and John— really see this person, even, or especially, if it inconvenienced me. Maybe the person would head to the temple courts, perhaps for the very first time, walking and jumping, and praising God. Maybe, in my giving, he would receive the overflow of God's love.

This is the heart of this book: the outlet—the releasing— of what God has given us to others. It's as simple as holding a conversation with the person who asks about the tee shirt you're wearing. And as difficult as remodeling your mindset and budget so you can release more. Generosity flows first from our hearts. Remember, because God first loved he gave. Generosity begins with a change in the heart. As we release what God has given us, we release the walking and jumping and praising God in others. And in so doing, our generosity comes back to us in the form of an abundant life, one filled with meaning, joy, and a deeper happiness that only God can give.

In the next chapter, I want to make a biblical case for enlarging our hearts, because until what is happening inside us changes, there can be no outlet. There will be only a Dead Sea.

For I testify that they gave as much as they (the Macedonians) were able, and even beyond their ability.

2 CORINTHIANS 8:3

It is never really about the amount of money or time that we give others. Instead, the heart of the matter is the joy that spills over into generosity. Generosity is a characteristic of people with joy. Generous people are joyful people.

CHAPTER 2

THE GENEROSITY MANDATE

am an entrepreneur, but I've felt the sting of unemployment. Years before I started Brewer Direct, I was between jobs in the mid-eighties for almost a year and received what seemed like unending months of unemployment checks before landing my next gig. I was committed to tithing, but the financial pressure raised the stakes:

Do I really need to tithe from this paltry unemployment check? I thought. *Hasn't this money already been taken out of my previous check—at least partially?*

The difference between my regular check from the job I had and the one from unemployment felt like a yawning chasm. I began to grapple with two fundamental questions: To whom does my wealth really belong? And, am I really compelled to be generous? I certainly wasn't wealthy. Maybe it was more accurate to say, "To whom do my paltry resources belong?"

Especially in times of anxiety about our financial futures, the question of generosity moves from the peripheral to the center of our thought processes: *Is generosity optional?* Several years after my first stretch of unemployment, I was unemployed again and wrestling with the same questions. But this time the decision to be generous was not as intense. I had finally grasped the larger truth about God's

Is generosity optional?

---

view of our resources. In this chapter, I want to build a biblical case for generosity, because before we can make decisions about our resources, we need to understand God's perspective on our wealth.

Generosity as Righteousness

In the Old Testament, the word *generosity* appears only eight times in the NIV (New International Version). There's no one Hebrew word to express the concept of generosity. In the Psalms, the word *hanan* is used. It means, "to show favor." In Psalm 37:21, for example, the text can be literally rendered, "the righteous show favor and give." The same word is also used in Psalm 37:26 and Psalm 112:5—the righteous or good people "show favor and lend."

A different expression is used in 2 Chronicles 31:5. The people of Israel are commanded to give a portion of their harvest to the priest. The Hebrew for "generously gave" is a form of the verb *rabah*, which means, "to make many or much." That is, they "gave much" in response to the command to give. In Proverbs 11:25, a "generous person" is a person of blessing (Hebrew *barakah*). And in Proverbs

22:9, "generous" people are literally rendered as "good eye" (*tov 'ayin*), an idiom for generosity.[17]

In the Old Testament, generosity is a signal of righteousness. To be generous is to be righteous. The opposite is, then, also true: the lack of generosity signals unrighteousness, something that is also associated with idolaters, fornicators, swindlers, murderers, and thieves. In *Generous Justice*, Timothy Keller argues that giving isn't charity. "In English…the word 'charity' conveys a good but optional activity," he writes. Instead, he says, the generosity God calls us to is more akin to "acts of righteousness."[18]

"Not giving generously, then," Keller writes, "is not stinginess, but unrighteousness, a violation of God's law."[19]

In a sense, the Old Testament views generosity holistically, as one part of the whole, the righteous life. Generosity is not mere tithing. Generosity is about one's larger

> *In the Old Testament, generosity is a signal of righteousness. To be generous is to be righteous.*

relationship to the Giver of all things.

In the article, "The Time Is Ripe for Radical Generosity," Dan Olson tells the story of R. G. LeTourneau, a 20th-century entrepreneur who was called the father of the earth-moving industry. As a 16-year-old, Mr. LeTourneau discovered faith at a revival meeting, and the decision shaped his giving behavior for the rest of his life. At some point, he made the decision to give away 90% of both his personal and corporate income to several non-profit organizations. You may be familiar with the name LeTourneau, because he founded LeTourneau University in Texas. But he also gave generously to other nonprofit organizations committed to advancing the kingdom of God in emerging economies, including countries in Africa and South America.

Someone asked Mr. LeTourneau about his generosity, and he said, "The question is not how much of my money I give to God, but rather how much of God's money I keep for myself."[20] It might be easy to dismiss the generosity of high net worth individuals like Mr. LeTourneau. You might be tempted to think:

> "I'd love to live on 10% of the enormous amount of money he made. It's not so hard to give away 90% when you're so wealthy."

As I mentioned in the previous chapter, more wealth does not necessarily equal bigger hearts or more largesse. The two are not correlated. What's most important is having the mindset of a righteous person. We need to know that all gifts—whether wealth, talent, time, or acquired skills—come from God, as is written in James 1:17. God owns the cattle on a thousand hills, as the Psalmist writes, and he is the originator of every good thing in our lives. God entrusts us with what he created and ultimately owns, which is what I came to understand in full as I tithed from my unemployment checks. As God's gifts increased, it might have been a greater temptation to fall into unrighteousness and hoard my resources. But I had learned what's "mine"—my proverbial cattle on a small hill—wasn't truly mine. What is mine is for me to release.

Generosity as Righting Inequity

Generosity is not just a signal of one's righteousness, however. It's also the way in which God rights a wrong world. It's how God creates good in the world. It's through the good gifts that God bestows on each of us that the world changes for the better. In *Christians in an Age of Wealth: A Biblical Theology of Stewardship,* New Testament professor Craig L. Blomberg writes,

> "Had Adam and Eve never fallen into sin, their descendants would have continued to enjoy paradise. Economic inequities, like all other injustices in the world, resulted from the fall, even if only indirectly. So we should not be surprised to see Abram and his elect offspring, through whom God's plan of redemption would emerge, beginning to model the redistribution of their wealth to those with fewer possessions than they."[21]

There are many Old Testament figures (Boaz, Solomon, and Nehemiah, to name just three) who redistributed their wealth for the good of those who had less. In the Book of Ruth, Boaz models what Blomberg calls the "generosity of the godly rich." Boaz allows Ruth, a foreigner, to glean extra in his field, enabling someone who is in poverty to work while she benefits from the generosity of the wealthy. Gleaning was an Old Testament custom mandated in Leviticus 19:19. Landowners were commanded not to harvest the fields right up to its edges, so the poor (widows and the elderly, for example) could survive. In obedience to God, Boaz contributes to the dignity of the poor by allowing them to work for their food.

One way that God provides for those suffering economically is through the generosity of those who call themselves people of faith. Today, we use the phrase "social justice." Blomberg writes, "Sometimes he [God] fulfills his promises supernaturally or through natural forces without human participation, but more commonly it is as his people share his concern and enact his will on earth that suffering of the afflicted is relieved, especially when they are his people."[22]

Many people I know support the efforts of organizations such as Compassion International or World Vision that care for poor children in emerging economies. For years, I've supported a child for $30 a month through an organization called World Harvest, and recently I had the chance to visit this boy and his family in Indonesia. I started supporting him when he was nine. He has a brother with Down syndrome, and his parents live in a cement building no bigger than the living room in my condo (and my living room is not large). I was overwhelmed with the warmth of this family. They wanted to go to Kentucky Fried Chicken, which has a franchise in the city near where they live, and so we did. Through a translator, I learned that the mother is praying for me, and her prayers and tears moved me so deeply. I left Indonesia feeling that I have been blessed by God to meet this family.

Generosity shrinks the inequity gap that causes so much human suffering in the world while also enlarging our understanding of God's uncontainable love for us.

The kingdom of God is truly upside down. In the economy of heaven, the poor in spirit are rich and in turn bless others. "Poor" is not necessarily poor in the economic sense but in humility. Often those who have much in this world are not humble but arrogant. Yet in God's economy, those who are humble in spirit have the most. God certainly didn't need me to provide for this family; he could have used any number of means. But by my extending God's love, small as it was, in the form of a $30 a month debit to my checking account, God returned his blessing to me through the prayers of this woman.

When we resist the temptation to serve money, and instead allow money to serve God's work in the world, we demonstrate divine love and move closer to where God's heart is at in the world. Generosity shrinks the inequity gap that causes so much human suffering in the world while also enlarging our understanding of God's uncontainable love for us.

Generosity as Overflowing Grace

In the words of one of the most quoted verses of Scripture, "God so loved the world that he gave his one and only son…" (John 3:16). In his work during three short years of earthly ministry, including sacrificing his life on the cross, Jesus did what he did because he was moved by compassion. And that is at the heart of generosity. The theology of generosity is

When we resist the temptation to serve money, and instead allow money to serve God's work in the world, we demonstrate divine love.

not as simple as "Give, and it will be given to you. A good measure, pressed down, shaken together and running over, will be poured into your lap" (Luke 6:36-38). It's not merely giving to get. The essence of generosity is that because God loved, he gave. The great gift of God is not money; it is a changed life that begins to overflow with gratitude.

In chapters eight and nine of 2 Corinthians, the writer, the apostle Paul, tells the story of the generosity of the Macedonians, an impoverished community that he lifts up for their sacrificial giving. It's clear Paul knew about the rivalry that simmered across the Grecian islands between the Corinthians and the Macedonians. Corinth was a port city, and Paul wrote the second book to Corinth after receiving word about division and sin in the church. Historically, Greece and Macedonia (called the "barbaric north") had a lengthy political rivalry with Achaia (Corinth) to the south. In 2 Corinthians 8:3-5, Paul writes,

"For I testify that they gave as much as they [the Macedonians] were able, and even beyond their ability. Entirely on their own, they urgently pleaded with us for the privilege of sharing in this service to the Lord's people. And they exceeded our expectations: They gave themselves first of all to the Lord, and then by the will of God also to us."

In the midst of extreme poverty, the overflowing joy of the Macedonians welled up in rich generosity. In the midst of economic hardship, the Macedonians garroted any excuses that we may have about generosity because money is tight. Out of deep affliction, they gave so others could live—and that the gospel of Christ might overflow to others.

As Scott J. Hafemann writes in *The NIV Application Commentary: 2 Corinthians*, "The collection, however, was more than simple charity. It had a theological purpose, both for the Corinthians and for the church as a whole."[23] Hafemann writes that the generosity of the Gentiles for the impoverished Jewish community in Jerusalem was a "tangible demonstration of the new covenant of the new creation (8:15).[24] Gentiles had given sacrificially to help Jews, through whom the spiritual blessings had come. The Gentiles had experienced the grace of God through Jesus, a Jewish man. And now the Jews were experiencing the grace of the God through the Macedonians, a Gentile community.

As I reflect on the profound generosity of that New Testament community, I am reminded that it is never really about the amount of money or time that we give others. Instead, the heart of the matter is the joy that spills over into generosity. Generous people are joyful people. Hafemann reminds us that, for the apostle Paul, the most important element of the gift of the Macedonians was not the idea of giving money to others. The key was that they had given their lives to God: "That the Macedonians gave themselves 'first' to the Lord is not a reference to a temporal sequence but to the priority of allegiance to God."[25]

Joy is the natural outflow of a life given over to God. And one of the markers of joy is generosity. So does generosity produce joy or does a joy-filled person tend to be generous? Probably both. It seems that the Macedonian's generosity amid suffering was an overflow of joy that came from putting God first. However, modern research also shows that generous people are happier people. In their book, *The Paradox of Generosity, Christian Smith and Hilary Davidson* write, "Happiness can be the result, not of spending more money on oneself, but rather of giving money away to others. General financial givers are happier people ..."[26] It's obvious from the passage that the Macedonians received a great blessing from God as a result of their generosity. I felt that when I visited the child whom I supported in Indonesia. I could not imagine the feeling of being blessed by that family. It's an emotion that is hard to describe and impossible to replicate without the letting go that comes with the act of giving. People who have what we call "generous spirits" have enlarged hearts. They are open and positive. Somehow their view of the world is that there is more rather than less. They are free not to cling anxiously to what they have. Contrast the story of the Macedonians with the findings from a recent study on generosity after America's Great Recession:

> We find consistent evidence that ungenerous life-styles associate with an apathy riddled by anxiety. Our interviews with Americans who do not practice generosity reveal that they are deeply unsettled by individual and social problems. Yet they don't think they have any obligation to respond, and even if they do, they feel inadequate to make a difference without sacrificing their ability to care for their own needs.[27]

The authors go on to argue that The Great Recession and the mortgage crisis strengthened the resolve of Americans to protect rather than share their assets. "Fear is a powerful motivator," write the authors, "and the fear of having too little, sometimes rooted in reality and sometimes fabricated or expanded, powerfully motivates them to protect their resources."[28] While I can empathize with the fear that drives this type of clinging—so was my initial inclination when I became unemployed—I am more fearful of clinging, or Dead Sea living, with no outflow. I have experienced firsthand "Sea of Galilee" living, and what an outlet can do to create joy in my life.

When I was unemployed the second time, the drought

lasted only six months. This time, I was settled in what I knew to be true—generosity is not an option, especially when times are hard. Somehow, I managed to make it through the days of fear and anxiety about my future. I didn't receive surprise checks, unexpected rebates, or returned overcharges from insurance. When I decided to give while struggling financially, I had to do some adjust-

> I have experienced firsthand "Sea of Galilee" living, and what an outlet can do to create joy in my life.

ing, and God always provided. I learned to give out of obedience. Not forced compulsion but from a loving act of surrender.

When we open our hearts, let go of what is in our hands, and remember that our lives, talents, and our treasures belong to God and are simply on loan to us, we are ready to experience the blessings of generosity. Suddenly, there is an outflow, just like the Sea of Galilee, a release that not only refreshes those downstream but the water (the life of the person) of the sea itself. I recently re-read the story of the feeding of the 5,000 in the Gospel of John, where a boy initiated the miracle of Jesus by handing over what he had. His gift was simply five barley loaves and two fish and, by Jesus' miracle, those "downstream" were greatly blessed.

As I'll discuss in greater detail in the next chapter, there are at least two principles of generosity to keep in mind about the generosity mandate. The first is that generosity produces joy for the person who lets go of his or her wealth. The second is just as important. It's that the grand blessing we can count on receiving as a result of being generous is the privilege of glorifying God. "Those who give generously of their surplus income," writes Dr. Craig Blomberg, "know from experience that in the vast majority of instances they do not recoup the money from other sources."[29]

That is, it's not really about the five barley loaves and two fishes. It's not that because the boy gave his lunch to Jesus, he will in the future receive tenfold what he gave in financial blessing. That may be true. That may not be true. The full measure of God's love is not merely financial blessing.

When we open our hearts, let go of what is in our hands, and remember that our lives, talents, and our treasures belong to God and are simply on loan to us, we are ready to experience the blessings of generosity.

It's much grander. Ultimately, our generosity is about the larger story of glorifying God:

"Because of the service by which you have proved yourselves, others will praise God for the obedience that accompanies your confession of the gospel of

Christ, and for your generosity in sharing with them and with everyone else. And in their prayers for you their hearts will go out to you, because of the surpassing grace God has given you. Thanks be to God for his indescribable gift!" (2 Corinthians 9:13-15)

As I look to the end of my life, no greater words could be spoken of me than those that were spoken of the Macedonians: someone whose generosity moved others a little closer to the grace of God. That's the story of God's uncontainable love. That's the story I want my life to tell.

*But when he saw
the multitudes, he was moved
with compassion on them,
because they fainted,
and were scattered abroad,
as sheep having no shepherd.*

MATTHEW 9:36

———————

This is the true
potential of generosity. When we
open our hearts and our hands—
remembering that our lives, our talents and our treasures are really on
loan to us— we are ready to create
the spillover effect of generosity.
In other words, you are ready to let
your love overflow—to release the
love that's been given.

CHAPTER 3

ENLARGING
THE HEART

t's often suffering or loss that initiates the journey to generosity.

An acquaintance recently told me a story about his son, a football player who as a senior in high school had high expectations for his future. The player was a nose tackle who had won his starting defensive position during summer football camp at a large suburban high school. During the first scrimmage of the season, he left the game because of an injury. He returned to health almost immediately but for a variety of reasons, including conflict with the coach, he didn't start a single game for the rest of the season. He played only limited minutes in each game.

He had hoped to play in college, but now he had little film to send to potential schools. "More than anything," he had said to his father, "I wanted to hear the announcer call out my name during the starting lineup for the game under the Friday night lights." But that would never happen in high school.

In the spring of his senior year, after almost giving up

on ever playing again, he finally found a small Division III school whose coach said he could try out for the team. For many Division III programs, making the team is no large feat; most everyone does. The issue, of course, is setting foot on the field on a Saturday afternoon. His first year, he wound up as the third string nose tackle, behind two players who were faster than he was off the line. After his freshman year, through a series of meetings with the coaches, he decided to move to the offensive line. That meant learning a new position and gaining about forty pounds. He worked hard the summer before his sophomore year and felt ready for the move.

A week into summer camp of his sophomore year, two weeks before the first game, a 300-pound lineman rolled up on his leg, snapping his fibula and wrecking the deltoid ligaments in his ankle. The transverse fracture required eight screws and two plates to repair. Football was over for his sophomore year and likely forever. The student fell into depression and almost dropped out of school during the first semester that year. He struggled simply to make it to class, first with a scooter and then with crutches. He began the tortuous and dreary road of rehabilitation.

At some point during the spring of his sophomore year, nine months after the fracture, he decided that he would give football one more shot. But something had changed. Of course, he still yearned to play every down on Saturdays, but that seemed highly unlikely. He would be learning a new position as a junior, since he had not yet had the chance to play offensive tackle. He had to decide whether he wanted to play for the love of the game and what was best for the team or simply give up altogether. It all sounds like a cliché, until one loses all hope for what you really want most. By the time he arrived at summer camp right before his junior year, he was back in shape, his leg and ankle rehabilitated enough to complete the drills. "My coaches had zero expectations of

> *You have to be broken*
> *before you can be given.*

---

me," he said. "I started out as third or fourth string offensive tackle." He ended his junior year, second only to the starting offensive tackle, even playing a few minutes in several games on Saturdays. During summer camp his senior year, however, he beat out a 310-pound lineman who was expected to be the starter at left tackle. The son of my acquaintance started every game his senior year of college.

This is a story not of achievement or even persistence. It is a story of loss. It is a story of what happens when the dream dies. It is the story of what rises from the ashes after all hope is gone. What emerges is not victory. What comes forth is a different perspective. No longer is it about the person.

You have to be broken before you can be given. When we're broken, we release control. We release our expectations. We release the white-knuckled grip we have on our lives. We open up. We're transformed. It echoes how Jesus broke the bread, was broken on the cross, and he gave. Jesus's body was broken, ultimately, to be released.

And for this young football player, every game became a gift, no matter whether he started. Even as a junior before he knew how his football years would end, he began mentoring younger players, changed his major to sports medicine and athletic training because of all the physical therapists and trainers who had assisted in his recovery, and

> *Jesus's body was broken, ultimately, to be released.*

found small places to serve on the team. He began helping other football players as they made their way back from injury. When his father would ask him about when he might have a chance to start, he'd reply, "Dad, it's not about that. It's about the team."

The darkness of the valley can enlarge our hearts for something greater than a life for ourselves. We experience a supernatural grace that comes from letting go. And in the grace emerges gratefulness and compassion, which must precede the kind of generosity that spills over to others. The heart enlarges. It wells up. It overflows.

Love after Loss

I grew up thinking I was never good enough. An unwanted child, I felt fundamentally tarnished, damaged goods. As I entered adulthood, I viewed myself as repulsive. In *Finding My Voice*, the memoir about my throat cancer, I use the metaphor of a leaky boat. For the first several decades of my life, I was adrift at sea, my little watercraft taking on water. I tried plugging the leak, with a patch of good works, a patch of material distractions, a patch of self-importance born from worldly success.

The boat kept taking on more and more water, however. No matter how fast or carefully I patched the holes, the makeshift fixes didn't hold, at least not for long.

Some of my leaks originated from my family system, in which my siblings and I experienced my parents' faith as the worst kind of fundamentalism. At home, we used the language of grace and love in how we talked about God, but ultimately, faith was less about a relationship with God through grace and more about a set of beliefs and

The darkness of the valley can enlarge our hearts for something greater than a life for ourselves. We experience a supernatural grace that comes from letting go.

rules to which we had to adhere, also known as "works righteousness." My parents struggled to create a family environment in which the children could develop a strong sense of self and confidence. We all ended up feeling not good enough, insufficient, less than. As I reflect upon my life and that of my siblings, I can see that as adults we each compensated differently, some in more destructive ways than others.

In addition to a growing up in the teeth of fundamentalism, I suffered from the malady common to other humans, what theologians and philosophers refer to as the God-shaped vacuum. French mathematician and philosopher Blaise Pascal characterized it as a "craving" for the "true happiness" once in man "that now remains [an] empty print and trace." Pascal writes that he or she "tries in vain to fill with everything around him, seeking in things that are not there the help he cannot find in those that are, though none can help, since this infinite abyss can be filled only with an infinite and immutable object—in other words, by God himself."[30] There is a faint memory, within each of us, of something deeply satisfying. As humans, we pursue many paths to reconstruct or create that happiness or "fill the vacuum" but with little success. As I made my way through my twenties and thirties, I filled mine with the pursuit of financial success, eventually starting a business that provided more financial resources

There is a faint memory, within each of us, of something deeply satisfying. As humans, we pursue many paths to reconstruct or create that happiness or "fill the vacuum" but with little success.

than I ever dreamed possible. Much about my pursuit, though, was largely about, to revert back to my original metaphor, patching my little one-person dinghy. It was nothing short of vanity. My life was about Randy. I had grown up in a family that made faith a part of its language and traditions, so I knew intellectually that the pursuit of so-called worldly things would create more holes than it filled, but I had to learn that in real time. I really had not made the connection that only God's love could permanently fill the emptiness. God's love was a childhood

> *It was then, at my most desperate moments, when Jesus showed up, sometimes by a sense of God's presence in times of solitude and at other times through the love of friends.*

abstract, not a living reality. I didn't feel love. I felt unloved and unlovable.

In midlife, I was diagnosed with a rare form of throat cancer. My very future was in jeopardy. And in those long and dark days I grappled with what it meant to be loved by God. It was then, at my most desperate moments, when Jesus showed up, sometimes by a sense of God's presence in times of solitude and at other times through the love of friends. It's hard even to write about without it sounding sensational, but Jesus didn't patch the leaks or help me bail out the water. He gave me a new boat—one with no holes, no leaks. And then he got inside the boat with me. Through a miraculous surgery and then recovery, I was able to talk again. My voice, my life, was saved. I was grateful for the outcome, but the dark night of the soul had fundamentally shifted how I saw myself. I had finally come to grips with the truth that no matter what happened to me, I was loved. I had discovered grace.

The Cross that Leads to Generosity

In the first chapter, I made the case that generosity began at the cross when God first loved us: "For God so loved the world that he gave his one and only Son, that whoever believes in him shall not perish but have eternal life" (John 3:16). Generosity flows from love. Consider these synonyms for "generous": lavish, magnanimous,

I had finally come to grips with the truth that no matter what happened to me, I was loved. I had discovered grace.

openhanded, bountiful, unselfish, ungrudging, free, and indulgent. So, too, God's love was lavish, magnanimous, openhanded, bountiful, and free in the incarnation and sacrifice of Christ. Multiple times God's love is described as so lavish and bountiful it overflows: "You, Lord, are forgiving and good, abounding in love to all who call to you." (Psalm 86:5) and "The Lord is gracious and compassionate, slow to anger and rich in love" (Psalm 145:8).

Throughout the Gospels, Jesus looks upon the mobs of hurting, sick, and searching people, and he wells up with compassion. Matthew 9:36 says, "When he saw the crowds, he had compassion on them, because they were harassed and helpless, like sheep without a shepherd" (Matthew 9:36). Later (see Matthew 15:32 and Mark 8:2), Jesus expresses his compassion for the lost again. It was this deep well of care that made the Word flesh and sent the Son to the cross. Christ's love overflowed at the cross in the ultimate act of generosity. His example demonstrates that generosity isn't earned. It isn't forced. It doesn't expect anything in return. It is an overflow of a compassionate heart.

It turns out that we humans, despite our self-preserving nature, have the capacity for compassion. A growing body of research supports that we have a "compassionate instinct," an idea first posited by Dacher Keltner, a psychology professor at University of California, Berkeley. In other words, compassion is as elemental to our survival as is what some people call our Darwinian (self-preserving) tendencies. A series of studies conducted by Daniel Batson, a professor and researcher from University of Kansas, found that compassion promotes altruism. According to Batson's studies, when humans encounter other humans in need or distress, they often imagine what their experience is like. Identifying another's perspective leads to empathic

Christ's love overflowed at the cross in the ultimate act of generosity.

concern that motivates actions that would enhance another's welfare, sometimes at the expense of one's own comfort and well-being.[31]

Batson conducted a series of experiments in which participants watched another person receive shocks when he or she failed a memory task. Participants were told that those receiving the shock had experienced shock trauma as a child. They were then asked if they would take shocks on behalf of the participant. Those participants who had reported feelings of compassion volunteered to endure several shocks for that person, even when they were free to leave the experiment. In another experiment, Batson studied if and how compassion prompts people to help someone in distress, even when their acts were completely anonymous. In this study female participants wrote notes to someone who expressed loneliness and an interest in spending time with the participant. Those participants feeling compassion stepped up to spend significant time with the other person, even when their act of kindness would remain anonymous.

Daniel Coleman, science journalist and author of the bestselling book *Emotional Intelligence*, agrees: humans have a natural propensity toward compassion. He explains how our "mirror neurons" are vehicles for us to "feel" with someone in need and make compassionate choices. However, he says in a TED talk, that when we are in a hurry—simply, when we are self-absorbed—our compassion wanes. Coleman cites the study of Princeton seminarians who studied the Good Samaritan and one by one were told to head to another building to deliver their sermons on this iconic story of compassion. As they walked to the building, each one passed a man bent over, moaning and clearly in pain. Though each of them was steeped in the story of the do-gooder, the only ones to stop and do good were those who felt they weren't in a hurry. If they were absorbed in delivering their sermon, they ignored the bystander. Coleman's conclusion? It's "the predicament of our lives: we don't take every opportunity to help because our focus is in the wrong direction."[32]

New Directions

Often, as the story of the football player and my story illustrate, only great suffering or loss can break through selfishness or wrong-headed thinking so that gratefulness and, ultimately, generosity can emerge. In my early adulthood, I was headed in the wrong direction (I felt like I was sinking, after all). I was headed down Randy Road. The heart is

> *Generosity begins with cultivating our heart. When we understand that we are loved, we can love. When we love, we give.*

fickle, deceitful, wicked, and as Scripture points out, it can't be trusted. It's also a gauge for how we will act, and when it is steeped in "me," it can't be filled with love for others. Jesus said, "For where your treasure is, there your heart will be also" (Matthew 6:21). When my boat was sinking, my heart was shriveled by a desire for power, fancy cars, success, and the good life; it was not focused on God, and, therefore, not on others.

Self-focus and me-centeredness keep us moving in the wrong direction. When we consider giving, we wrestle with the fear of giving away too much. We can rationalize our lack of generosity by saying, "What if I am not able to pay my bills? What if something unexpected comes up later this week or later this month?" Some people live paycheck to paycheck, weighed down by debt so that giving seems impossible. Still others have the means but are fearful of compromising their standard of living. In his book *Crazy Love: Overwhelmed by a Relentless God* Francis Chan writes, "Lukewarm people give money to charity and to the church as long as it doesn't impinge on their standard of living."[33] Opposite of the day-by-day provision that Scripture promises in passages like Matthew 6, we allow fear to dictate how much we give, and how much we hoard.

It's nearly impossible to overcome such fear on our own by trying harder. Generosity begins with cultivating our heart. When we understand that we are loved, we can love. When we love, we give. Generosity can never flourish out of compulsion or manipulation. Philip Yancey, author of *Where Is God When It Hurts* and *The Jesus I Never Knew,* writes, "There is but one true Giver in the universe; all else are debtors."[34] To become more generous is to receive God's love. To follow God's example, it only makes sense that all of us debtors live similarly generous lives. Like the inlet and outlet of Sea of Galilee, we both receive and give. As Paul writes in 2 Corinthians 9:8, "And God is able to bless you abundantly, so that in all things at all times, having all that you need, you will abound in every good work." Notice Paul doesn't say that we will overflow in every good offering and tithe. Generosity is much larger than money; it includes how we use our time and even our general outlook, and our spirit toward others.

No one would say Mother Teresa was financially

prosperous. But many would say she is among the greatest of all givers. She once said, "Let us not be satisfied with just giving money. Money is not enough, money can be got, but

Generosity begins with an awakening to the grace of God and then wells up and spills over into the lives of others.

they need your hearts to love them. So, spread your love everywhere you go."[35] Generosity is not directly correlated to wealth. (In fact, I've pointed out in previous chapters that wealth might actually hinder generosity.) Generosity begins with an awakening to the grace of God and then wells up and spills over into the lives of others.

Compounding Generosity

Years ago the movie *Pay It Forward*, starring Helen Hunt and Haley Joel Osment, popularized a new language for giving. In the movie, a young boy attempts to make the world a better place with a charitable program based on the networking of good deeds. The recipient of the favor does a favor for three others rather than paying the favor back. The concept is ancient, first used as a key plot element in a 317 BC Greek play. In his 1841 essay "Compassion," Ralph Waldo Emerson spoke to this ideal when he wrote, "In the order of nature we cannot render benefits to those from whom we receive them, or only seldom. But the benefit we receive must be rendered again, line for line, deed for deed, cent for cent, to somebody." The phrase was coined by Lily Hardy Hammond in her 1916 book *Garden of Delight*, when she wrote, "You don't pay love back; you pay it forward."

This is exactly what happened at a McDonald's drive-thru in Scottsburg, Indiana on Father's Day 2017. It started when a woman, paying for her meal at the cashier's window, noticed a dad with small kids in the car behind her. The store manager says of the lady, "She looked back and saw a father with four little kids, with a couple of Happy Meals. She said she was going to pay for him, and to tell him Happy Father's Day."[36]

Her $36 act of generosity spilled over and into the heart of the father, who proceeded to purchase the meals for a few cars that followed him. For nearly four hours, from 8:30 p.m. to midnight, every driver paid it forward. Drive-thru cashier Hunter Hostetler ushered in the generosity—161 cars' worth.

"I had people telling me," he says, "'No, it's going to stop here. It's going to stop at 100. You're not going to make it past.'"

But generosity continued to spill over. The "161st customer, Abby Smith, said, "I thought it was pretty amazing. You don't see a lot of pay-it-forwards anymore." At one point a customer threatened to stop the wave of generosity, but the McDonald's staff pooled their own money to keep it going. And generosity would have kept going had the store not needed to close. The final customer wanted to keep it going.

"We had to tell her we were so sorry, and we needed to

close," Hammon said. "But it would have gone further."

In the New Testament story, the boy who gave Jesus his five barley loaves and two fish to feed the multitudes responded generously, and the generosity spilled over. One commentary notes, "Jesus provided 'as much as they wanted' (John 6:11), and 'they all ate and were satisfied' (Matthew 14:20). Christ did not just meet the need; he lavished them with so much food that there were "twelve baskets full of broken pieces and of the fish" left over (Mark 6:43).

This is the true potential of generosity. When we open our hearts and our hands, remembering that our lives, our

I wanted to live out the reality that had come alive within me.

talents, and our treasures are really on loan to us, we are ready to create the spillover effect of generosity. In other words, you are ready to let your love overflow and to release the love that's been given.

My first bout with cancer reoriented my life. When asked by a close friend, "Now what?" following the successful surgery, I said, "I want to help people around the world." It wasn't merely about good works. I wanted to live out the reality that had come alive within me. I began pouring myself into mission work globally. When God's love was unleashed inside of me, I was able to unleash love to the world. Generosity is not just writing a check or pulling out your wallet. It is about enlarging ones' heart and unleashing God's love for the world. Our unleashing creates a pay-it-forward effect, and, like the Sea of Galilee, the good in our lives begins to flow outward to others.

One of my overflows is to help underprivileged children and young adults across Africa and Asia. In addition to mentorship, I specifically like to support higher education and fund entrepreneurs with start-up capital. My intent is

> *Generosity is not just writing a check or pulling out your wallet. It is about enlarging ones' heart and unleashing God's love for the world.*

that the gift will multiply. For instance, I met a group of young African men who created a business plan for audio rental at weddings, worship services, and graduations. The plan had promise, but they lacked one critical component to making the business work: equipment (and the capital to purchase what they needed). I assisted the young team with their equipment needs. I wanted them to become self-sustaining, so they too could begin to pour their lives into the community and their families. Each month I check in, asking, "How much money have you produced?" From an American's perspective, $1500 a month in revenue isn't much, but it's paying for the four of them, all their transportation, books for school, food, and shelter. I gave one gift and now it's multiplying. It released potential.

Christian author Randy Alcorn has said that if you have a heart for something, you should invest in it. To illustrate, he explains that if you invest in Google, you closely follow Google. Amid the sea of tech companies, the one you are concerned about is Google—because you are invested in Google. Similarly, if you invest in the kingdom of God, your heart grows for the things of the God's kingdom. Of course, if you invest in Google, the motivation is often the net monetary return. In the kingdom of God, the return is most often not monetary, though there is data that indicates that generosity correlates with financial security, which I will discuss in Chapter 4. The return might also be mental and physical well-being, which I will discuss in Chapters 5 and 6. Whatever the tangible returns, the intangible return is experiencing the fullness of God's love. When you release God's love, you receive God's love. When have an outlet, you experience the abundant life.

Give, and it will be given to you. . . . For with the measure you use, it will be measured to you.

LUKE 6:38

While I believe in this "give and you'll receive principle," we often limit God when we define his generosity in solely temporal terms. All the treasures amassed on earth, we are reminded in Matthew 6, are ephemeral. Ultimately, they don't satisfy our eternal longings.

CHAPTER 4

RELEASING FINANCIAL BENEFITS

H ad I, as a six-year-old boy, the inclination to hold onto the quarter my father gave me instead of dropping it into the offering basket, it would have grown into quite a tidy sum by this point. Of course, that assumes I would have had the foresight and discipline to save, add to, and then invest that money throughout my childhood. Instead, I gave the quarter away. I released it.

I can't take credit for my behavior at six years old. But it was a good impulse. And it has served as a model throughout my life, enriching my life in immeasurable ways. One way is financial. I'm going to step out on limb in this chapter and say that practicing generosity has also made me financially better off. That statement comes with some strong caveats.

I'm at a moment in life where I have chosen to give away much of my income. I don't want to add to my net worth.

My desire is to release my time and resources continually so that, when my life is over, I will have spent what I've been given in order to empower others. In my case, as a single man without children, I don't see the value of leaving behind an impressive sum of money at the end of life. How would that do anyone any good? In Philippians 2:17, Paul compares his life to a drink offering: "But even if I am being poured out like a drink offering on the sacrifice and service coming from your faith, I am glad and rejoice with

Listening well can be a radically generous act.

all of you." As I accumulate time on this earth, I seek to pour out what I've been given.

As discussed in the previous chapters, generosity and loss often—if not always—go hand in hand. When we make *any* kind of contribution, engage in *any* act of generosity—whether it's giving away our attention, money, or other resources—we lose something. When we give our full focus to the people with whom we come into contact, for instance, even if we meet them one day and will never see them again, we're being generous ... and we're making a trade-off. By giving someone else our undivided attention, we're making a choice. We choose not to focus on ourselves, not to promote our own ideas or agendas, and not to distract or entertain ourselves on our phones or in any other way. Instead, we slow down and honor someone else's story. And I can attest to the fact, after listening to people all over the globe, many people don't have *anyone* who truly listens to them. Listening well can be a radically generous act.

Whether as substantial as investing a large part of your income in a ministry or as minor as replacing worn running shoes for a homeless man you see on your way to work, when we make a financial donation, we surrender opportunities or a sense of security if we'd kept that money. But, again, although giving away money involves loss, what we gain is far greater than what we lose.

I propose in this chapter that generous people tend to be wealthier than their more cautious, fearful, or tight-fisted peers. I say this with trepidation. While I believe that in God's economy, he seeks to bless us as we are faithful to bless others, I also understand that what it means to be "blessed" has been wrongly shaped by the world in which wealth is synonymous with happiness. While our wealth might increase, what is more important is that, in the act of being generous, we are released from the burden of more: more money, more stuff. We come to realize that true treasure is found when our heart is centered on God and not when we are pursuing *more*.

Get Rich Detour

Before we look at how generous people are often wealthier, including financially, than those who do not prioritize giving, I'd like to examine how this truth can be misconstrued. The "prosperity gospel" is the basic idea that material blessings are directly correlated to one's faith. One core assumption of this belief is that it is God's will for us to be prosperous. It turns spirituality into a financial transaction: If you have enough faith, and give sacrificially to God, you will receive more money than you need or can even manage. Some TV evangelists make frequent requests for their audiences and congregations to give sacrificially to the church, promising that God, in return, will make their wildest material dreams come true. They'll be "blessed."

These blessings, of course, have little or nothing to do with forgiveness or redemption or the abundant life Jesus referenced in John 10:10. The abundance that those who

> *While our wealth might increase,*
> *what is more important is that,*
> *in the act of being generous, we are*
> *released from the burden of more:*
> *more money, more stuff.*

believe in the prosperity gospel seek instead has everything to do with enjoying a lifestyle—houses, vacations, and cars—fit for celebrities or royalty.

Unlike Jesus' words (recorded in Luke 20, among other places) that the poor are "blessed" because the kingdom of God is theirs or his statement that "...the last will be first, and the first will be last" (Matthew 20:16), the prosperity gospel says you are meant to be the head, not the tail. You are meant to be the owner of the business, not just an employee. That car you're driving should turn heads, not just get you from point A to B. The prosperity gospel defines abundance in a narrow way, a material way. Consider the context of the Sermon on the Mount. Jesus was speaking to the poor, outcast, downtrodden, oppressed. They were desperately seeking relief from the Jewish leaders (Pharisees and Sadducees) as well as the Romans. At their core, they were seeking relief, not a promise of material prosperity. Jesus said in Matthew 6:25-34, "Consider the lilies of the field or the birds of the air...they don't focus on what to eat or how to live, God takes care of them." So, too, we need to not focus on the "stuff," but on God's provision.

Some people use Jeremiah 29:11 as biblical support of the idea that God cares about us having more worldly wealth: "'For I know the plans I have for you,' declares the LORD, 'plans to prosper you and not to harm you, plans to give you hope and a future.'" While these words are comforting and speak to the character of God, it's important to remember that they must be looked at in the larger context of God's relationship with Israel. Jeremiah is speaking for God to the Israelites, who have been long-lost in exile, and reminding them of a future *not* in exile, promised years ago. Using scripture, such as this, as proof that wealth is a sign of God's favor is dangerous. The broader application of that passage is that God is aware of our suffering and that even when things seem chaotic or dire, God is working with us and within us.

Generosity, then, isn't transactional but transformational. God wants us to be conformed into the image of Christ and to experience the peace and joy that, ultimately, accompanies such a transformation.

Time and time again in scripture Jesus speaks to the ills that come with a pursuit or love of material stuff. Matthew 6:33 says for us to seek the Kingdom first. We're to seek things like peace, forgiveness, sacrifice, compassion, kindness, and generosity. God is less concerned about our bank accounts growing and more interested in our hearts growing in kingdom values. In Luke 6:38, Jesus says, "Give,

> *Generosity, then, isn't transactional but transformational. God wants us to be conformed into the image of Christ and to experience the peace and joy that, ultimately, accompanies such a transformation.*

and it will be given to you. A good measure, pressed down, shaken together and running over, will be poured into your lap. For with the measure you use, it will be measured to you." While I believe in this "give and you'll receive principle," we often limit God when we define his generosity in solely temporal terms. All the treasures amassed on earth, we are reminded in Matthew 6, are ephemeral. Ultimately, they don't satisfy our eternal longings.

The false hope of financial prosperity is not what I

endorse. In fact, this superstitious conflation of luck and a limited view of God disturbs me. But I've seen it all over the world. And we are all prone to it. Those who live in poverty cling to it out of desperation because their basic needs for food and shelter are unmet. The "rich" grasp it out of the fear that they might lose what they have worked so hard to gain. Or they feel deeply insecure about how they came to accumulate such wealth. Both groups maintain a scarcity mindset when they put their faith in the prosperity gospel, a sad misunderstanding of God's desire to bless us in many aspects of our lives, not merely our finances.

The late Mother Teresa, whom I mentioned in the previous chapter as an example of someone living prosperously, spent the majority of her life living among the unprivileged, ministering to the poor in Calcutta. When she received the Nobel Peace Prize in 1979 for her life of service, she refused the banquet typically given in honor of the winner. Instead, she asked that the money that would be spent on the event—amounting around $192K—be given to India's impoverished. Mother Teresa did not die wealthy, but who could ever say Mother Teresa wasn't rich? Even while she never tapped her own resources for the conveniences of life, she was blessed and, dare I say, prosperous. This is a much more complete view of real generosity and the benefits of prosperity.

The prosperity gospel also has a sinister, often unspoken, underside: If you believe health and wealth are a sign of God's favor, then poverty and illness must be a sign of God's condemnation. Jesus refutes this idea in John 9:1-5 when he gives sight to a man who had been born blind. The disciples were certain that the man was blind because either he or his parents had sinned. They didn't ask *whether* his blindness was punishment for sin, but simply wanted clarity about *who* had sinned and caused this disability. Jesus said that neither the man nor his parents sinned, and he healed the man. The Pharisees then accused the now sighted man of "being steeped in sin at birth" (John 9:34), but Jesus says that those who think of themselves as seeing are blind and that the blind see. Jesus makes clear that he's

What I know for certain is that God is with me. No matter what I go through, I will still be his.

come to bring light to the world, and the Pharisees miss the light that is right before them.

To write her book *Blessed: A History of the American Prosperity Gospel*[37], author and Duke University professor Kate Bowler spent ten years traveling across North America interviewing pastors and congregants who adhere to the "health and wealth gospel." She dug into the history of the prosperity gospel, finding that this form of American Christianity—one of the most popular today—is rooted in part in a late 19th-century movement called "New Thought." New Thought was an early form of positive psychology that urged people to use their minds to bring about health and material wealth in their lives. This movement dovetailed with the emerging notion of the

American Dream, which promised that ordinary people—by keeping positive and working hard—could escape from poverty and achieve wealth and fame far beyond their humble origins.

Like me, Bowler has received a life-altering diagnosis of cancer. Like me, she lives with the knowledge that her time on earth is limited. Some days I feel like I'll live forever; on others I struggle with pain and discomfort. But, in addition to all of this and maybe most importantly, like me, Bowler feels blessed by God and understands that the absence of health (or wealth) does not mean God is missing. Like me, she knows that sin hasn't caused her illness and knows that God does indeed have a plan for her future. Like me, while she lives with the symptoms of her illness and side effects of her treatment, she has hope.

In her more recent book, *Everything Happens for a Reason: And Other Lies I've Loved,* Bowler writes,

> What would it mean for Christians to give up that little piece of the American Dream that says, 'You are limitless'? Everything is not possible. The mighty kingdom of God is not yet here. What if 'rich' did not have to mean 'wealthy', and 'whole' did not have to mean 'healed'? What if being the people of 'the gospel' meant that we are simply people with good news? God is here. We are loved. It is enough. [38]

It *is* enough, and I believe in healing, even while living with my cancer diagnosis. But I believe that our ultimate healing is way beyond this life. I pray that Jesus will heal me on this planet and ask for it all the time, but even if he doesn't, I'll serve him anyway. What I know for certain is that God is with me. No matter what I go through, I will still be his.

Generosity's Riches

The value of generosity is not that it produces wealth. Our sole focus should be on the fact that when we are generous, we release God's blessings to others. It's not about us.

There are, however, some blessings that correlate with generosity. We, indeed, grow rich with the insight that God's economy is different than the world's economy. We grow rich in humility by learning to trust God rather than rely on our own resources. We grow rich in gratitude. Our hearts are enlarged, and we grow into generous spirits. Later, I'll share some research that does suggest that generous people can also be more financially affluent. But, for me, that's not the point of giving with an open, whole-hearted attitude.

In some ways, we could sum up Bowler's words about giving up that "little piece of the American Dream" by saying that God's economy is very different—and far greater—than the economy of earth. When we chalk up the work God is doing in the world and reduce it to a financial transaction, we miss the point. I could make a case to say that God's economy is upside down, just the reverse of how the world's economy works. As we read in the Sermon on the Mount and elsewhere, the poor in spirit are actually rich.

That's upside down! In the Parable of the Lost Sheep, Jesus asks those listening—an eclectic group of tax collectors, Pharisees, and sinners—who among them wouldn't leave 99 of their sheep to find the single one that was lost (Luke 15:1-7)? That's upside down, too. God's economy is different from our own. God seeks out that last, lost sheep.

> *When you are affluent, you can begin to believe that you are the master of your life, that you can control everything that happens because you have the resources to take care of yourself.*

Jesus' words about how hard it is for a rich man to enter the kingdom of heaven also reveal God's attitude toward the love of money. As told in Matthew 19:24; Mark 10:25; and Luke 18:25, Jesus says that it's "easier for a camel to go through the eye of a needle than for a rich person to enter the kingdom of God." Jesus says, "Again, I tell you." It's like he's saying, "For the hundredth time, I'll repeat…" It's easy to minimize what this passage is actually expressing; many reduce it to "As long as I'm tithing the bare minimum, it's okay to be wealthy." But it's less about what one is giving, and more about the *freedom* one experiences in giving.

Think back to the rich young ruler whom Jesus instructed to give away everything in order to walk with him. Instead, the rich man walked away from Christ. He'd allowed his wealth and resources to master him, rather than mastering his own resources. His wealth held him captive.

When you are affluent, you can begin to believe that you are the master of your life, that you can control everything that happens because you have the resources to take care of yourself, buy yourself out of trouble, and steer your life in whatever direction you choose. With great wealth, people can make varied and spectacular attempts—with possessions, experiences, or other things—to fill the "God-shaped vacuum" that Pascal described. But those who are "poor in spirit," maybe especially those who are financially poor, are unable to rely on their own resources. They must humbly approach and trust God to patch up their leaky souls. They must be vulnerable, ask for help, and see themselves as woven into a community instead of somehow being above it or detached from others.

If any person could have "named it and claimed it," it would have been Jesus. Christ himself asked his Father to "take the cup of suffering" from him, but God said, "No." Despite his fear and suffering, Jesus humbled himself and said, "Not my will, but yours be done." It's this kind of submission that ultimately brings lasting happiness. In the journal *Science*[39], Dr. Elizabeth Dunn, a psychology professor at the University of British Columbia, gives evidence of the fact that spending money on other people is a more effective "route to happiness" than spending money on oneself. Dr. Dunn has performed many academic studies of how "time, money, and technology shape human happiness" and is the co-author of *Happy Money: The Science of Happier Spending.* She warns readers against mindless, acquisitive spending. In contrast to giving, buying happiness leaves us empty. It doesn't fill that God-shaped hole. "We are happy with things," Dunn writes, "until we find out there are better things available." It's a restless, never-ending pursuit. But generosity promotes happiness.

People who are generous givers also have an increased sense that they are wealthy, as Zoë Chance of Yale University and Michael Norton of Harvard Business School showed in a study published in *Advances in Consumer Research.* Generous people feel subjectively more affluent, regardless of what's in their bank accounts.[40]

"We propose that philanthropy may have an unintentional self-signaling effect—when we observe ourselves making charitable donations, we infer we must be prosperous," Chance and Norton write.[41]

There is, however, also research to support the idea that those who are generous with their material wealth often enjoy more *actual,* not subjective, financial security and affluence than those who cling to their resources. Part of this has to do with careful maintenance of one's finances, releasing ourselves from mindless spending and consumption and the debt that usually accompany them, and having a proper appreciation for what we possess.

But there is more to it than that. A study discussed in an article titled "Giving Makes You Rich" in *Entrepreneur* magazine[42] reports that evidence "supports the contention that giving stimulates prosperity...Charity, it appears, can really make you rich." The article looks at whether the reason for this is metaphysical—Does God bless us? Is the so-called "Law of Attraction" at play?—or if this phenomenon can be explained by other factors.

While a definitive explanation of why giving "makes you rich" isn't given, the article concludes that giving and wealth "mutually reinforce each other" as "economic growth pushes up charitable giving, and charitable giving pushes up economic growth."

More data, also cited in the article, collected from The Social Capital Community Benchmark Survey (SCCBS) supports the idea that there is a corollary between giving and increased wealth, specifically that the richer you are the more you give. That's not surprising. If you have more wealth, you're able to give away more money. But social scientist and president of the American Enterprise Institute, Arthur C. Brooks, analyzed the data to identify if wealth actually increases as you give more. It would be easy to point to the mega-rich, like Warren Buffet whose net worth increased in one year (2012-2013) from $44 billion to $54 billion after he donated $3.084 billion in the same year period. But what about the everyday family? Brooks concluded from his study that a family that gave away $100 more than another family in the same income bracket will predictably earn, on average, $375 more.[43]

Such studies might be used arbitrarily to support a purely transactional rationale for generosity, that I, at the outset of this chapter, refuted. The point is not that we should perform generous acts in order to receive something in return. I think we can say with some confidence, however, that we will receive some measure of financial benefit when we give with open, loving hands to others. Our meter for generosity goes up. And, as we continue to release what we've been given, our gratitude can prevent us from striving after acquiring more things. We may become more content and manage our resources better. When we choose not

> *So, although giving away money or other resources represents loss, ultimately what we gain is far more than what we lose.*

to grasp our possessions with fisted hands, but instead hold our resources lightly and keep the palms of our hands open to share God's blessings, those same open hands are also ready to receive God's blessings and live life to the fullest. So, although giving away money or other resources represents loss, ultimately what we gain is far more than what we lose.

Proverbs 11:24-26 reads, "One person gives freely, yet gains even more; another withholds unduly, but comes to poverty. A generous person will prosper; whoever refreshes others will be refreshed." The wisdom of the Old Testament is echoed by Jesus in his telling of the Parable of the Talents in Matthew 25. Three servants were entrusted with varying amounts of wealth: to one he gave five bags of gold; to another he gave two bags of gold; and to yet another he gave one bag of gold. None were told what to do with the money. Of the three, two invested wisely, multiplying the wealth they were given for their master. But the other buried what was given, too fearful to invest. While the first two servants are commended—and put in charge of more wealth—the other is scolded. As a parable, the gold is synonymous with so much more than mere wealth. It's a metaphor for everything—gifts, time, and treasure—that God has entrusted to us. The motivation here isn't that the servant will grow his personal wealth, but that the kingdom of the Master is increased. In being part of that increase, the two servants experience joy, freedom, and increased opportunity to invest. In giving, they receive.

And it is in giving we receive, too—so much more than simply more treasure on earth.

Remember this: Whoever sows sparingly will also reap sparingly, and whoever sows generously will also reap generously ... for God loves a cheerful giver.

2 CORINTHIANS 9:6-7

Y ou know the old maxim, "God loves a cheerful giver?" When we give, we reflect God's character. We accomplish just what we were created to do. And, we're rewarded with true happiness. Being a giver truly does makes us happy.

CHAPTER 5

RELEASING PSYCHOLOGICAL BENEFITS

This past December, my team at Brewer Direct, the marketing agency that I founded, got me the perfect Christmas gift. If you're guessing it wasn't a watch or any other kind of gadget, you're right! Not an exotic vacation weekend or a night out at my favorite restaurant either.

My team sponsored a child in Indonesia in my name. That special gift showed me how much they understand me. They know what makes me tick. What some of them might *not* have known, however, is that their gift echoes something I did years ago after I made my first trip to Africa, specifically to Rwanda and Kenya. I hadn't gone to Africa because I loved the continent or its people. I'd traveled for a much more pragmatic reason. At the time, I was serving on the board for a Christian organization in the US, and the board chair invited me to attend a once-every-three-years ministry gathering. We met, discussed our agenda, and even went on safari. But what engaged my heart was making a visit to a children's school and home outside of Nairobi, not far from one of Kenya's biggest slums. The campus wasn't posh by any means, but it gave kids a proper place to live. They had access to adequate sanitation, meals, and a safe place to sleep. And they were obviously grateful.

When I got back home that November, America was gearing up for Christmas. Trees flashing with colored

I'd been moved to action, out of compassion.

lights. Santa decorations everywhere. Crèches on every church lawn. Christmas music nonstop. The kind of energy that comes from a culture anticipating a holiday.

I was still in culture shock after my short stint in some of the worst poverty of the world. I told my circle of colleagues and friends that I was canceling Christmas. That is, the significant sum of money I usually spent on gifts would be redirected. It would go to support kids in the slums in Africa. And I didn't want anyone spending money on me, either. It all needed to go toward lifting kids out of dire situations.

I'd been moved to action, out of compassion. And we were able to donate several thousand dollars that year. That was the best gift I could imagine. Author Kay Warren, wife of Pastor Rick Warren of Saddleback Church, had a similar life-changing moment in relation to suffering in Africa. Rick Warren says that it began when Kay happened on an article in Newsweek.[44] She learned, in that ordinary and yet fateful moment, about the AIDS pandemic in Africa. AIDS has left tens of millions of children orphaned. Putting down the magazine, she noted to her husband that she'd had no idea. At the time, she had never even met one orphan. She was stunned. God broke her heart, and she was moved to act.

Later Rick Warren would feel his heart break, too, over the global orphan crisis. They would then get engaged— really engaged—in serving AIDS orphans. Kay founded Orphan Care Initiative and continues to find sponsors for orphans in Rwanda and elsewhere. The "gift of generosity," Kay Warren's website simply states, "is impacting multiple generations."[45]

Like the Warrens, on my first trip to Africa—and on every subsequent trip—I let my heart break over that which breaks God's heart. And that inspired me to give generously to people in need in Africa. As I often say, though, you don't have to travel to an African country or to Indonesia or anywhere else to practice generosity. It's not about getting on a plane. But you do have to open your eyes. And open your heart. And while it might be a broken heart that compels you to practice generosity, something else occurs. Something that heals and makes us more whole. The benefits of practicing generosity, as I've explored throughout this book, can be spiritual and even financial. But there's more. A growing field of research shows that practicing generosity also secures incredible psychological benefits. But don't take my word for it. There's neuroscience to back me up.

Brains Lighting Up

A study conducted by Dr. Soyoung Q. Park, a psychologist, and her colleagues that was reported in the journal *Nature Communications* reveals the "neural link between generosity and happiness."[46] In the study, participants were given money. Members of the control group were told to spend it on themselves. The experimental group promised to spend it on others. Researchers found that participants in the experimental group grew in generosity over the course of the study. They made more and more decisions

A growing field of research shows that practicing generosity also secures incredible psychological benefits.

to give to others. They also were found to be much happier than the control group who spent the money on their own wants and needs.

Park and her team used M.R.I. imaging to track how the brain responded when participants in the experimental, generous group committed to give money to others. These study subjects' brains actually looked different than those in the control group. Their brains behaved differently. When people committed to giving money away, scans showed the temporo-parietal junction—a region of the brain associated with altruism—lighting up with activity. That part of the brain then communicated with the ventral striatum, or the brain's reward center. In plain English for the nonscientists among us, when we practice generosity, our brains are changed. And they reward us with feelings of happiness.[47]

Park and her colleagues looked at several kinds of motives for generous behavior, including maintaining a positive reputation and supporting one's family. However, they concluded that these have "limited explanatory power for the pervasive propensity of humans to be generous in different settings."[48] They proposed an evolutionary explanation for why generosity affects us on the neural level. They postulate that early humans may not have worked well in community or pooled their resources had their brains not rewarded them with these good feelings when they shared. Because, as I've established in this book, generosity usually—if not always—involves loss. So, what would motivate primitive people to extend generosity and give away precious, hard-won resources if it weren't for the positive feeling of happiness that they gained? The same is true for us today.

Created to be Generous

You'll remember that, in Chapter 3, I introduced you to the work of Daniel Coleman. It is Coleman who claims that human beings have a natural propensity for compassion. While we've seen how researchers examine this "natural propensity" from psychological, neurological, and even evolutionary perspectives, as a believer, I would assert that the brain "lights up" when we're generous because we were actually created by God to give.

Genesis 1:26 begins, "Then God said, 'Let us make mankind in our image, in our likeness…'" Theologians over the centuries have been captivated by the concept of "Imago Dei," or that humans are made in the image of God. Countless scholars have attempted to nail down just what it means. Some say it's our ability and desire to create—art, music, literature—that reveals that we're made in (our Creator) God's image. Others say it's that we can discern the difference between right and wrong. Another interesting school of thought connects humankind's desire for rela-

I believe we were created to reflect God's heart, God's character. And that the truest thing about God is that God is love.

tionship with the doctrine of the Trinity. We are made for relationship, it posits, because we are made in the image of a God who is ever in relationship. We reflect a God who lovingly exists in three distinct persons, these theologians maintain.

In his book *The Weight of Glory*, C.S. Lewis reflected on Imago Dei. He marveled at how even the "dullest, most uninteresting person" reflects God's glorious image. We might meet that person in God's presence someday and be dazzled by his or her immortal beauty. Lewis wrote,

"It is in the light of these overwhelming possibilities, it is with the awe and the circumspection proper to them, that we should conduct all of our dealings with one another, all friendships, all loves, all play, all politics. There are no ordinary people. You have never talked to a mere mortal."[49] Instead, Lewis reminds us, you and I are always interacting with someone who bears God's exquisite image.

All of these reflections on what it means to be made in the image of God intrigue me. But, for our purposes here, I'd like to look at how being made in the image of something means we reflect or mirror what is most true about it. Down to our core. I believe we were created to reflect God's heart, God's character. And that the truest thing about God is that God *is* love.

When asked what is the greatest commandment, Jesus had a ready and very clear response. "Love the Lord your God with all your heart and with all your soul and with all your mind.' This is the first and greatest commandment. And the second is like it: 'Love your neighbor as yourself'" (Matthew 22:36-40). If our God-ordained *purpose* is to love others, it seems clear that we were indeed *created* to be generous.

Some studies even suggest that just thinking about God promotes "positive social behavior and generosity to strangers." In one study whose results were published in the journal *Psychological Science,* two groups of people were asked to play games involving unscrambling words and phrases. One group was "primed" to think about "god concepts." Their games included words or concepts related to God, including "spirit," "divine," "sacred," and "God." And, whether or not they identified as believers, these group members went on to practice cooperation and generosity. In the control group, participants were given non-spiritual words to unscramble. After the game, members of both groups were given money and asked to decide how much to keep and how much to donate to anonymous recipients. Overwhelmingly, the participants in the "spiritual words" group donated more money than the others, 68 percent to 22 percent. The study's principal researcher wrote:

> We did not anticipate … simply getting partici-
> pants to unscramble sentences with a few key words,
> having such a large effect on people's willingness to
> give money to strangers.[50]

We've been created by a loving God to love others. And it's well to remember—to echo Lewis's statement—there are no ordinary people. We are all made in God's image. And by aligning with who we've been made to be, we enjoy real psychological benefits.

Giving of Our Time and Talents

It's not just being generous with our money that makes our brains light up and reward us with a feeling of happiness. We were created to give, too, of our time and resources. Countless studies show the psychological benefits of serving others.

For example, Dr. Francesca Borgonovi, a Research Fellow

at the London School of Economics, published a study in the academic journal *Social Science and Medicine* that showed that people who volunteer report far greater happiness than people who do not. Regardless of the level of affluence of the volunteers and non-volunteers, those who performed "voluntary labor for religious groups and organizations" were

People who cling to their time, money, and other resources—locked in a fearful embrace with self-preservation—miss out.

happier. Borgonovi writes, "We propose that volunteering might contribute to happiness levels by increasing empathic emotions, shifting aspirations and by moving the salient reference group in subjective evaluations of relative positions from the relatively better-off to the relatively worse-off."[51]

Americans who describe themselves as "very happy" volunteer an average of 5.8 hours per month, according to Christian Smith and Hilary Davidson, a statistic cited in their book, *The Paradox of Generosity*.[52] Giving of one's time also provides people with a sense of purpose. This, of course, makes perfect sense if we believe that we were actually *created* to love others.

People who cling to their time, money, and other resources—locked in a fearful embrace with self-preservation—miss out. Their brains' reward centers aren't lighting up. They miss out on God's blessings, as did the third servant in the Parable of the Talents whom I discussed in the previous chapter. They aren't aligned with the people God made them to be. And they miss out on experiencing the happiness that generosity generates. Their chests are tight. They're nervous, stressed. Instead of generating happiness, they hold fast to fear. But when you give, you're like a tree growing along a flowing river. You bloom. You flourish. You live life fully.

A Cheerful Giver

You know the old maxim, "God loves a cheerful giver?" We've established in this chapter some reasons why this is true. When we give, we reflect God's character. We accomplish just what we were created to do. And, we're rewarded with true happiness. Being a giver truly does makes us happy. But that pithy little phrase?

In 2 Corinthians 9:6-7, the Apostle Paul writes,

> Remember this: Whoever sows sparingly will also reap sparingly, and whoever sows generously will also reap generously. Each of you should give what you have decided in your heart to give, not reluctantly or under compulsion, for God loves a cheerful giver.

And that whole-hearted, open-handed giving—yes, you might even call it "cheerfulness"—will have a positive effect on us at a neural level.

Orphan Mansion

A few months after graduating from college in the early 1950s, a man we'll call Robert landed his dream job as an industrial arts high school teacher. As a side hustle to his day job, he decided to try to build a house. It took almost two years, but eventually he put in the final nail, and he and his new wife moved in. Then a year later, he decided to build another. He then sold the house they had just built— and moved into the next.

By his mid-twenties, Robert left his teaching job and made the shift into homebuilding full-time. And, for the next four decades, he amassed a fortune building houses for the baby boomers in one of the fastest growing suburban areas of the United States. At about the time his only son joined the business in the early 1990s, Robert took his first mission trip to Africa, something he had avoided for years. Perhaps he was simply too busy. Perhaps it was easier to avoid the suffering of the world. The homes that he had spent his lifetime building were ones only the upper middle class could afford. Some of them might even be called "McMansions," a derisive term coined in the 1980s by architects and architecture critics in response to the trend of unnecessarily big, poorly designed, very expensive houses being built in American suburbs.

The first trip to one of the western African countries crushed him. Earlier, I used the phrase "it broke my heart" in reference to how a similar experience affected me. Perhaps that phrase is a little too cliché. Robert was devastated. He was not prepared for the great beauty of the people juxtaposed with their abject poverty, especially that of the orphaned children who foraged in garbage dumps for survival.

Within a year after his first trip to Africa, Robert set up a foundation and took his home-building crew to the country to construct an orphanage. Over the next twenty years, Robert and a group of missionaries ran an orphanage that transformed not only the lives of the children in the village but the economics of the village itself.

If you asked Robert's wife, Sue, she would say that Robert got a new lease on life in his mid-sixties when he first started traveling to Africa. No more was he amassing treasures on earth but in heaven. The biblical truth, "Whoever sows sparingly will also reap sparingly, and whoever sows

> *When we are generous, joy is released in our lives and our capacity for more abundance and happiness increases.*

generously will also reap generously" (2 Corinthians 9:6) was true for Robert. In the final years of his life, he sowed generously and he reaped a life of purpose and joy, what Jesus calls the abundant life. His passion for generosity drove him to travel even into his early eighties, when his family thought he should stop.

Generosity and its benefits are not just for uber-wealthy business people, of course. It's the joy of a family who adopts a child. It's the joy of working shoulder to shoulder with others on a home for a family devasted by a hurricane. It's the joy of a teenager visiting the neighbor who is shut in. It's the joy of a college student tutoring. It's the joy of paying for the burgers and fries of the family behind you in the drive-thru line.

When we are generous, joy is released in our lives and our capacity for more abundance and happiness increases. And this, of course, is why my team's Christmas gift of the child sponsorship meant so much more to me than any *thing* they could have given me.

For my thoughts are not your thoughts, neither are your ways my ways, declares the Lord.

ISAIAH 55:8

———

I'm not spending my remaining time on this earth wondering why it is that, even though I have lived a life of generosity, I have cancer. It's an unanswerable question. Life, obviously, is steeped in mystery. God's ways, as we all learn at some point in this life, aren't always our ways.

CHAPTER 6

RELEASING PHYSICAL BENEFITS

Opening my hands and giving generously to others hasn't protected me from suffering. Far from it.

As I write, I'm again living with cancer. And it's a cancer that's growing. I know there is no cure. I've been told what I can expect as it takes over my body. It will choke out the oxygen in my lungs, and, if it is not stopped, eventually I won't be able to breathe. I won't lie: when I was taking a trial medication, I was in pain. I can't pretend the cancer isn't there. When I'm at my physical worst, I simply can't do what I have in my heart to do. I have had to cut down on meetings, travel, and the work I love. In those dark moments, I sometimes pray, "God, what in the world are you doing?" But I do trust God is using the disease for my good and the good of the kingdom. And I know that even though I'm going through a fire, I won't be set ablaze.

Even now, I still feel blessed.

I've worked to maintain a posture of generosity over the course of my life, but I've never felt *entitled* to financial security or good health. As I asserted in Chapter 3, the so-called "prosperity gospel" is a misunderstanding of God's blessings and work in us. Generosity should never

> *I know that even though I'm going through a fire, I won't be set ablaze.*

be practiced with the hope that, in return, God will give us something back. Instead, as 1 Timothy 6:17-19 tells us, we should give generously to "take hold of the life that is truly life." That's deeper and more mysterious than a hollow, self-motivated transaction.

Even in my illness, even when I can't do as much as I'd like to serve others, I feel myself taking hold of the life that's "truly life." Part of that is holding fast to gratitude. I'm grateful for all the joy I've experienced in my life. Much of it has been the result of having a reason to get up every day. A sense of purpose. I'm grateful that my legacy will be one of giving, not stockpiling. And I have an ongoing and even growing sense of gratitude for God's presence with me. In fact, cancer has made me experience my faith in a much more personal way as I give myself over to God more and more deeply.

All to say, I'm not spending my remaining time on this earth wondering why it is that, even though I have lived a life of generosity, I have cancer. It's an unanswerable question. Life, obviously, is steeped in mystery. God's ways, as we all learn at some point in this life, aren't always our ways. Isaiah 55:8 reads, "For my thoughts are not your thoughts, neither are your ways my ways, declares the Lord." Amen!

The Health Benefits of Happiness

Despite my own particular illness, however, I maintain that there is a strong relationship between generosity and physical health. I can't argue with all the research, as well as what I've witnessed in others. Scientific findings confirm again and again that people who give generously of their time, talent, and financial resources are more likely to enjoy physical health than those who don't. Of course, as in anything, there are exceptions. There are many factors outside of our control—ones unrelated to our level of

Life, obviously, is steeped in mystery. God's ways, as we all learn at some point in this life, aren't always our ways.

compassion—that contribute to disease. We live in a fallen world in which accidents happen, toxins exist, and genetics aren't always favorable. All the same, in this chapter, I want to explore how open-hearted generosity can benefit your physical well-being. It's my wish for you that you'll give from an open heart, hold fast to the life that is truly life, and enjoy a healthy life.

Let's begin by backtracking a bit. In the previous chapter, we looked at how generosity affects our brains. When we give our time, financial resources, or attention to someone else, we're changed at a neural level. When we love like that, we're obeying the biblical injunction to live in harmony with everyone else (Romans 12:16) and to bear one another's burdens (Galatians 6:2). In fact, as I claimed in Chapter 5, we're being exactly the people God created us to be. When we're generous, our bodies respond from the core. We feel a lightness in the chest and even a warm glow. Our moods improve. In short, we experience happiness. (I'm glad to report that this wonderful effect can even happen when a person is battling a severe illness.)

While experiencing this kind of "natural high" may seem like reward enough for our generosity, we reap even more benefits when we give. Physical ones. That is, after our brains "light up," that happiness causes other parts of our bodies to change, too. Dr. Sara Konrath is a social psychologist and professor of philanthropic studies at Indiana University. An expert on the health implications of generosity and other prosocial behaviors, she's conducted extensive research and literature reviews on how giving time and money away positively affects our health. Giving to others, she has found, lowers morbidity—or the condition of being diseased—and "predicts reduced mortality risk."[53]

"There is a large body of literature finding that giving to others is associated with a number of physical health benefits for givers," Konrath writes, "including stronger immune systems, a reduced risk of serious illnesses, and a lower mortality risk."[54] Konrath reports that people who give financial and emotional support to others experience "faster recovery from depressive symptoms, reduced symptoms of inflammation," and better general physical health.[55] But why is this so?

One explanation is that when people give of their time and money, they often expand their social networks. And people who enjoy strong bonds with family and friends tend to be much healthier than those who are socially isolated. They exercise more. They are better suited to handle stress. They engage in activities that stimulate, rather than stagnate, the brain.

In trying further to puzzle out how exactly and why health improves when we give, Konrath and her colleagues looked at subjects on the biological level. They examined how stress-reducing hormones, such as oxytocin, are released when we experience the kind of happiness that giving—not receiving—generates in us. Even *thinking* about committing a generous act or remembering a time when we've been generous has the same hormonal effect. It reduces stress levels. And when it comes down to it, much illness and disease is caused by stress.[56]

Stress Makes Us Sick

Heart disease is the leading cause of death for Americans. And, according to the World Health Organization, cardiovascular diseases—or "CVDs"—are also "the number one cause of death globally: more people die annually from CVDs than from any other cause."[57]

And what causes CVDs? The American Heart Association reports that chronic stress affects "behaviors and factors that increase heart disease risk: high blood pressure and cholesterol levels, smoking, physical inactivity and overeating." Artery walls are damaged when people self-medicate, by drinking too much alcohol or smoking to manage their stress. The AHA states that the "body's response to stress may be a headache, back strain, or stomach pains. Stress can also zap your energy, wreak havoc on your sleep and make you feel cranky, forgetful and out of control."[58]

When we experience a stressful situation, adrenaline in the body is released. This hormone, unlike the oxytocin that calms us down and fills us with a sense of happiness and contentment, speeds up the heart. It makes blood pressure go up. Some people, when faced with a situation that makes them feel stressed or angry, say that they "see red." This surge of energy and focus is called the "fight or flight response." Mayo Clinic staff report that "when you encounter a perceived threat—such as a large dog barking at you during your morning walk—your hypothalamus, a tiny region at your brain's base, sets off an alarm system in your body. Through a combination of nerve and hormonal signals, this system prompts your adrenal glands, located atop your kidneys, to release a surge of hormones, including adrenaline and cortisol."[59]

Our bodies were made to handle sudden, high-pressure crises in this way: hormone levels surge, the situation is addressed, and then hormones go back to normal. The problem is, too many people live with elevated stress levels.

All the time. And the body suffers. When we live with constant stress, we become ill with disorders including depression, anxiety, personality disorders, cardiovascular disease, high blood pressure, abnormal heart rhythms, heart attacks, and stroke.[60]

In a list of ways to escape the problems stemming from chronic stress, doctors recommend eating a healthy diet, exercising, and getting enough sleep. But you might be sur-

The problem is, too many people live with elevated stress levels. All the time. And the body suffers.

prised at another common medical suggestion. Many physicians tell stressed-out patients to look outward: to focus on others. That includes giving time, talent, and money to people in need. They've found that spending time and money on others can be as effective at lowering blood pressure and reducing stress as medication or exercise.

One recent study published in *Psychology and Aging* tracked two sets of older adults. One group volunteered for four hours a week for 12 weeks, the other didn't. Four years later, the participants' blood pressure was measured against the baseline blood pressure readings taken before the experiment. Those who volunteered developed lower blood pressure.[61] What doctors have found, from their medical or biological points of view, is what we've explored in this book from other perspectives: Generosity lights up the brain and makes us happier and healthier. Practicing generosity is what we were created to do. It mirrors the God in whose image we were made.

A Story about an Onion

As you have surely learned after reading the first several chapters of this book, my work has taken me all over the globe. When I think of my travels and the generosity that has been shown to me—as well as the privilege of having

> *They've found that spending time and money on others can be as effective at lowering blood pressure and reducing stress as medication or exercise.*

been able to show generosity to others—I experience that warm glow that scientists and neurologists work so hard to explain. And I see, in person and over and over again, how a generous spirit can add not only life to a person's years, but years to a person's life.

A few years ago, for example, I made my first trip to the beautiful country of Vietnam. One day I visited a rural village market. The people in that remote place were not financially affluent by any measure. They worked as farmers, fishermen, and cooks, and this market was a vital part of the community. Their make-shift stalls were stacked with pyramids of gleaming fruits and vegetables. The fish they'd caught only minutes or hours before—including the heads!—were fresher than any seafood you'll find in a grocery store. There were homemade noodles and all manner of street foods for sale. The aromas of all of this fresh, carefully harvested and presented food was amazing.

Even more beautiful than all of the sights and smells was the spirit of generosity and kindness that filled the market. Not only were merchants gentle and kind to one another and to their regular customers, but they were welcoming to me, a stranger in their midst. As I passed by each merchant, I was warmly offered samples. My guide translated for me, and I can't count how many friendly expressions of welcome I received that day. I remember thinking, *It's no wonder that people in cultures like this live well into their 90s and even past 100 years of age.* Their spirits of generosity just shone. Again, I left those cross-cultural exchanges a better, happier, and more whole person.

One of the vegetables that was sold at that market was called *he* (pronounced "hey"). It's similar to an onion and is often used in soups. And, if you've been to Vietnam or to a good Vietnamese restaurant, you'll know that the country is famous for its soup. There's a story about that vegetable that moves me. I'll get to it later, but first I want to share a bit about the author, Thich Nhat Hanh, a global spiritual leader and Buddhist monk. Now 92 years old, he is famous for his teachings on mindfulness, or the practice of living happily "in the present moment." Mindfulness, as you might have noticed, is all the rage in our stressed-out culture. What might surprise you is that, throughout his speaking and writing life, Hanh has spoken with deep admiration about Jesus. No, he doesn't embrace Christianity, but he can't help seeing something very potent and unique in the person of Christ.

He proposes that, for Christians as well as people of other or no religions, Jesus can be upheld as a model of mindfulness and commitment to serving others. Jesus was fully present with the people around him. He took time for quiet meditation. He lived a life of service for others, ultimately giving his very life in order to release humanity from our sin.

Perhaps Hanh's friendship with the Catholic monk Thomas Merton, whom he met at The Abbey of Our Lady

Jesus was fully present with the people around him. He took time for quiet meditation. He lived a life of service for others, ultimately giving his very life in order to release humanity from our sin.

of Gethsemani in Kentucky in 1966, ignited his interest in Christ. Merton wrote much about the spiritual importance of generosity. In his book, *Seasons of Celebration*, he wrote, "Fear narrows the little entrance of our heart. It shrinks up our capacity to love. It freezes up our power to give ourselves."[62]

Many Christian laypeople and theologians, including Merton when he was living, have appreciated Hanh's reflections on Christ. His message to Christians that mindful contemplation can be a way for us to reduce stress, expand our hearts, and connect with the Holy Spirit—or God's "healing presence" as Hanh calls it—is powerful.

A famous anecdote that Hanh has often used to extol the virtue of generosity features that onion, or *he*, that I first saw at the market. He writes, "There is a kind of vegetable in Vietnam called *he* (pronounced "hey"). It belongs to the onion family and looks like a scallion, and it is very good in soup. The more you cut the plants at the base, the more they grow. If you don't cut them they won't grow very much. But if you cut them often, right at the base of the stalk, they grow bigger and bigger." He claims that the same is true when we practice generosity. "If you give and continue to give, you become richer and richer all the time, richer in terms of happiness and well-being. This may seem strange but it is always true."[63]

The idea of being cut at the base and, in some mysterious way, growing, packs a powerful punch for me at this moment of my life. I feel like, in what can only be described as strange, I'm both being cut back and growing stronger.

I thank God that it's so.

For we brought nothing into the world, and we can take nothing out of it.

1 TIMOTHY 6:17

Our problem is not our wealth. It's our reliance on it and our pride in amassing it. We are self-made, self-reliant, and self-obsessed. Our wealth often reinforces this. And we reinforce our wealth to stave off loss, not realizing that it's loss that opens our hearts to receive all good things as a gift from God, who provides us with everything to enjoy.

CHAPTER 7

GENEROSITY'S GREAT MYSTERY

Many years ago, I began sponsoring a boy named Chris in Kenya. When Chris was nine years old, well before I got involved in his life, he had to care for himself and his six-year-old brother, Peter. They had no other family. By sundown every day, they felt wrenching hunger. That's when they went "night hunting." People in their village cooked all day in big brass pots. At dusk they poured water in the pots, letting them soak outside overnight to loosen up the encrusted food. Every night Chris scraped the food from the bottom of the pots. It was the only food he and Peter ate.

The small amount of support I provided, along with help from others, lifted Chris and Peter out of mere survival into poverty. By our standards, it doesn't seem like much of an economic bump. But for them, it was a move from death to life. They suddenly had a future to live for and the energy to pursue it. Chris went to school, then on to college to get a degree in financial management. He now lives off his meager income from a small landscaping business. Chris doesn't have the income to provide much money to his impoverished neighbors, so he gives of himself, helping them in any way he can. He is now 29 years old and applying to graduate schools all over the world. He wants to be a leader and a person of influence in his community, Nairobi, Kenya. Peter, too, went on to college and is hoping to do great things after graduation.

My intervention, a small thing for me, helped move Chris and Peter from a state of continual stress into a state of safety. Chris was able to direct his energies and attention on moving forward and helping others. To use a biblical metaphor, Chris was rescued from the kingdom of darkness and transferred into the kingdom of light. That light revealed the stark contrast between his previous and his current condition and prompted a response of sheer gratitude in him, releasing his generosity.

In this chapter I want to look at our motives for giving. Not *what* we give, but *why* we do it. Chris's story helps us understand that it's not giving itself that brings us joy; it's what prompts the giving. 2 Corinthians 9:7 tells us that each of us must give as we have purposed in our hearts, not grudgingly or under compulsion, for God loves a cheerful giver. Our intervention helped change Chris's life, but it didn't change his heart. His gratitude did.

In Luke 17, Jesus heals ten lepers and rescues them from a liminal life as outcasts of society. All of the lepers went on their way, but only one stopped, saw that he was healed, and turned back. He realized what Jesus had done for him, and overwhelmed by gratitude, he came back and fell at Jesus' feet. Jesus said to him, "Were not all ten cleansed? Where are the other nine?" He then said, "Rise and go; your faith has made you well" (Luke 17:17-19).

Chris is that leper who returned in gratitude. Our relationship has grown to the point now where he calls me "Dad." "I'm just trying to follow after you, Dad," Chris tells me. "I want to give as you gave to me." Giving people are grateful people first. Gratitude begets generosity. And Chris has become one of the most generous people I know, giving completely of himself to his community.

The Many Motivations of Giving

"The principle of give and take; that is diplomacy—give one and take ten," Mark Twain once famously quipped.[64] Our motives for giving are a mixed bag. When we give, we

No one gives with entirely pure motives. We often give for selfish reasons, but that doesn't negate the goodness of giving.

also take, though rarely in the proportion Twain cynically asserts. When we give, how much do we get? How much of our ego rides on our giving? These are questions of motive.

No one gives with entirely pure motives. We often give for selfish reasons, but that doesn't negate the goodness of giving. It just means that we need to work towards a purer motivation and give with a deeper sense of gratitude for what we already have. Looking at our motives helps us understand how generous we truly are. And understanding our motives for giving helps us know how to become better givers. If we want to change a behavior, we need to get to the underlying motives for that behavior.

One of the very basic—and selfish—motives of giving can be found in the practice of reciprocity. Human relationships are built on reciprocity, an exchange, a give and take. Tit-for-tat. Scratch my back, and I'll scratch yours. Reciprocity's inherent selfishness is perhaps most revealed in the way we exchange gifts. In a fascinating study of violence in society, Renee Girard observes the strict protocol of gift giving:

> Prudence requires a no less strict equivalence in the giving of gifts than in the bartering of goods. Each party must imitate the other as closely as possible, while at the same time giving an impression of spontaneity. Each must convince the other that, in selecting the gift he gives him, he has obeyed an irresistible impulse, a sudden inspiration uncontaminated by the petty-minded calculations of ordinary people.[65]

To reciprocate means you give an equivalent—not a superior—gift. If you give a better and more expensive gift, it appears you are trying to humiliate or obligate the other person.

In Japan, I have observed the more negative effects of tit-for-tat giving. An entire industry has emerged around

"Omiyage," or souvenir giving. Every train station has a store or kiosk where you can buy the perfect gift, wrapped and bagged and ready to share with your family member, colleague, or host. This gift-giving culture has, in my experience, extended to favors. For example, my Japanese

We have our equivalent of "Omiyage" in our culture. It's called Christmas, when giving becomes an obligation and many go into debt doing it.

friend and host one time went out of his way to show me around his city, secured great seats for me at a baseball game as well as a soccer match, and treated me to a terrific meal. So, when he asked me to meet one of his friends at LAX and show him around and basically play host, I couldn't say no.

But of course, this doesn't even the score. If I do a good job, and the friend comes home with glowing reports, *both* my original friend and the guest who visited Los Angeles are now in my debt. And it goes around and around like this. We have our equivalent of "Omiyage" in our culture. It's called Christmas, when giving becomes an obligation and many go into debt doing it. If we give out of duty, if we seek reciprocity, if we hope we'll look good to others, or if we give in order to feel good about ourselves, our motives are messed up. We can give more and more…and become less and less generous. These distorted motives make us lose the joy of giving.

If we trace the motives for giving over the generations in America, we can get a better sense of what inspired our forefathers to give and how we, perhaps, need to return to some of the same qualities of devotion and sacrifice. America is becoming a wealthier and less generous nation, and our children have been labeled the "Entitled Generation."

Coming out of the hardship of the Great Depression, the ascendency of Roosevelt's New Deal, and the sacrifices

I encourage parents to send their children to places in the world where they can see the poverty in right in front of them.

of WWII, the Greatest Generation understood the meaning of devotion to country and the ideals which inspired America to become a great nation: democracy, freedom, and a feeling of destiny. This inspired gratitude while instilling a sense of duty, commitment, and an obligation to give back. The boomers capitalized on this, and generated prosperity that their parents could only dream of. The decades of peace that followed enabled boomers to draw that wealth inward. We became the biggest consumer economy in the world. We became triumphalist and rich.

The millennials who have followed are conflicted. They want to renounce the materialism of their parents and pursue the ideals that helped make this country a "city upon a hill," but they lack the sense of duty and responsibility that made it so. The Generosity Project found that "Givers are significantly more likely to give because they've been blessed than because they hope to receive a blessing. This is especially true of millennials, 89% of whom say, "I've been blessed to give back."[66] However, another report on motivation for giving from the Barna Group found that millennials perceive themselves as generous, yet they give less than other demographic groups.

Millennials tend to be motivated by causes, and constant interaction with social media campaigns tends to heighten and perpetuate a perception of involvement. But this involvement can be shallow and ephemeral. Motivation is often about appearances, presenting a good face on Facebook and racking up "Likes" for a contribution to a GoFundMe campaign. "Here's looking at me" has become our social media motto. When our phone has become our portal to the world and our focus is on maintaining our image on social media, there's little direct involvement with actual people to whom we can demonstrate real, hand's-on compassion.

This is why I encourage parents to send their children to places in the world where they can see the poverty in right in front of them. One such place is Kibera, the largest urban slum in Africa. Located in Nairobi, Kenya's capital, Kibera houses about 250,000 people who live on less than $1 a day and lack access to clean water and sanitation.[67] Closer to home, across the border in Mexico, we find millions of people living in slums where gang violence and drug use run rampant.[68] Getting involved with organizations dedicated to helping differentiate human beings from the 35-acre trash heaps they live on can only deepen one's motives for giving. It can change a heart.

Givers, Takers, and Matchers

In his book *Give and Take: A Revolutionary Approach to Success*, Adam Grant argues that success depends heavily on how we approach our interactions with other people. Grant asks the question, "Every time we interact with another person at work, we have a choice to make: do we try to claim as much value as we can, or contribute value without worrying about what we receive in return?"[69] Grant states that we pursue success using three different behavioral styles. *Takers* like to get more than they give. "If I don't look out for myself first," takers think, "no one else will." *Givers* are a relatively rare breed who prefer to give more than they get. Takers help others strategically; benefits outweigh the personal costs. Givers help whenever the benefits to others exceed the personal costs. A third category, *Matchers*, strive to preserve an equal balance of giving and getting. They believe in tit-for-tat, with relationships governed by an even exchange of favors.

None of this is surprising, but Grant goes on to say that the research demonstrates a startling reality. While givers often sink to the bottom of the success ladder, ultimately they rise to the top. They intentionally choose to "give" their way up the ladder. He writes:

> The answer is less about raw talent or aptitude, and more about the strategies givers use and the

choices they make. ... We all have goals for our own individual achievements, and it turns out that successful givers are every bit as ambitious as takers and matchers. They simply have a different way of pursuing their goals.[70]

Most powerful of all, however, is the way success spreads outward. "There's something distinctive that happens when givers succeed," Grant writes. "It spreads and cascades. When takers win, there's usually someone else who loses...but givers succeed in a way that creates a ripple effect, enhancing the success of people around them."[71]

Combined with their motivation, ability, and opportunity, givers create a synergy of success that elevates others. They don't use giving as a strategy as much as they simply strive to be generous in sharing their time, energy, knowledge, skills, ideas, and connections with other people who can benefit from them. In other words, they give of themselves in a way that transcends personal gain. And it continues to ripple outward. This is a powerful and purifying motivator, particularly when a person can give without any thought of taking, simply because they have everything.

Bill Gates is such a giver who has parlayed his ability and opportunity into a software empire that has made him billions of dollars and benefited billions of people. Not content to simply be successful and help others succeed, Gates gives away 50% of his wealth to help elevate the well-being of some of the world's poorest people through his global education and health initiatives. I don't know if God's love compels Bill Gates to help people, but I am sure that God is involved in his work. Any project that elevates the human condition is certainly blessed of God. Another mega-giver is Indian billionaire Azim Premji. In 2013, Premji became the first Indian billionaire to sign the Giving Pledge. Created by Gates and Warren Buffet, the Giving Pledge "encourages wealthy individuals to pledge half their fortunes to philanthropy." People like Premji—who is famously frugal—see themselves as "trustees" of their wealth. They see it as rightfully belonging to the larger community. According to Ingrid Srinath, one of India's leading proponents of strategic philanthropy, "generosity is…linked to a way of seeing the world and your role in it. It certainly has nothing to do with how much money you have."[72]

On a much smaller scale, I have experienced the same joy of giving to help others succeed and experience a better quality of life, sometimes in the most pedestrian of ways. I visited a church in Africa three times in the past decade, and after enduring their bathrooms—a step beneath our modern Porta-Potties—I decided to buy them new toilets. For $8,000 dollars, a small fortune in Africa, they will put toilets into all the bathrooms. This is more than an indulgence for a squeamish white man. The organization African Enterprise conducts crusades in African slums, and they also install sanitary toilets, one toilet for 2,500 people. There is something to say for being there, to sharing in their experiences and suffering. You won't be moved to help unless you have entered into their world and have sat on their bathroom squatters until your leg muscles scream.

A Purer Motivation

While there are financial, psychological, and physical benefits from generosity—that's not the motive for generosity, ultimately. It's often difficult, though, to know, fully, why we give. But as we become more generous, we are better able to sort out the "whys."

> *It's often difficult, though, to know, fully, why we give. But as we become more generous, we are better able to sort out the "whys."*

I have argued in this book that generosity flows only when it has an inlet and an outlet. That flow keeps the channel clear. It purifies. I return to my African friend, Chris. Our small monetary support created the inflow, and Chris's gratitude formed the outlet. While Chris was disadvantaged by his extreme poverty, it was his poverty that also enabled him to receive with gratitude.

Those who have nothing are in a position to receive. Most Americans are blessed and cursed by prosperity. We devote our attention to a sophisticated inlet system that we have created. Ironically, this puts us in a position not to receive but to take. It's no wonder that we don't freely give; we have not freely received. Even our charity is more often an expression of our benevolence rather than our gratitude or compassion.

Paradoxically, we need to arrive at the place where Chris started: with nothing. This is why I believe that loss is so important. It opens the outlet that is blocked by all that we have amassed. As I have stated, loss opens and enlarges our hearts for something greater than a life for ourselves. It creates space for us to be dependent on God and others, and it focuses our attention on the things that have eternal value. Our problem is not our wealth. It's our reliance on it and our pride in amassing it. We are self-made, self-reliant, and self-obsessed. Our wealth often reinforces this. And we reinforce our wealth to stave off loss, not realizing that it's loss that opens our hearts to receive all good things as a gift from God, who provides us with everything to enjoy (1 Timothy 6:17).

> *This book is not about giving, per se. It's about the purifying flow of generosity in our lives.*

This book is not about giving, per se. It's about the purifying flow of generosity in our lives. We can give—even enormous sums—without being generous. But we can't be generous and not give. Giving is a byproduct of our generosity. As I pointed out earlier, the story of the widow's two mites in the gospel of Luke is instructive. She gave two coins, a paltry sum—but it was all she had. Out of her poverty she gave everything. That's generosity. For Jesus, the value of the gift is not the amount given, but the cost to the giver; not how much is given, but how much is kept for oneself. It's the same for Chris who gives liberally of himself, although he has little.

In his book *The Prodigal God*, Tim Keller illustrates it
this way:

Once upon a time there was a gardener who grew
an enormous carrot. So, he took it to his king and
said, "My Lord, this is the greatest carrot I've ever
grown or ever will grow. Therefore, I want to present it to you as a token of my love and respect for
you." The king was touched and discerned the man's
heart, so as [the gardener] turned to go, the king
said, "Wait! You are clearly a good steward of the
earth. I own a plot of land right next to yours. I want
to give it to you freely as a gift so you can garden
it all." The gardener was amazed and delighted and
went home rejoicing. But there was a nobleman at
the king's court who overheard all this. And he said,
"My! If that is what you get for a carrot—what if you
gave the king something better?" So, the next day
the nobleman came before the king and he was leading a handsome black stallion. He bowed low and
said, "My lord, I breed horses and this is the greatest
horse I have ever bred or ever will. Therefore, I want
to present it to you as a token of my love and respect
for you." But the king discerned his heart and said
thank you, and took the horse and merely dismissed
him. The nobleman was perplexed. So, the king said,
"Let me explain. That gardener was giving me the
carrot, but you were giving yourself the horse."[73]

Our motives for giving are never entirely pure, of course, because it's impossible to divorce our ego from our giving. Whether we give out of duty, seeking reciprocity, desiring to look good to others, or to feel good about ourselves, our selves are always invested in our giving. But we can grow in our generosity as giving becomes less about us and more about the recipient.

The Giving Tug of War

Becoming generous is an ongoing work of the heart. And that work always creates tension between our desire to grasp and our willingness to let go. I liken it to a tug of war between our selfish nature and our giving nature. It's also a tug of war with our resources. We love our money, because our money represents security (or at least provides the illusion of safety). It's the story of the rich fool in the Bible, who stockpiles more and more grain in his barns, believing that his wealth will secure his safety. He had no tug of war. He was as oblivious to his greed as he was to his imminent death.

This harkens back to our instinct for self-preservation, our primal need to feel safe as we navigate a dangerous world. However, we also crave social engagement and trusting relationships. We want to protect ourselves but also give of ourselves to others, and we are happier when we do so. This is why we love the story of Ebenezer Scrooge, whose Christmas stinginess didn't ultimately lead to his happiness and fulfillment. We identify with old Scrooge, who typifies this tug of war between our uncharitable tendencies and the satisfaction we can ultimately derive from helping others.

How do we suppress our inner Scrooge? We don't automatically become generous. It takes intention and choice, as we develop habits and patterns of giving that increase the flow of generosity through our lives. Even our spontaneous giving—five dollars to the homeless woman who stands on the corner downtown—is more often prompted by a twinge of guilt than by a generous heart. Spending that five dollars helps me walk away feeling better about myself.

Becoming generous is an ongoing work of the heart.

Impulsive giving might assuage our guilt just a bit, but it doesn't open the heart. But we can employ strategies that nudge us to become more generous. Behavioral economists suggest that we make a concrete plan to give and set a specific goal for how much to give, to whom we'll donate, and when we'll do it. We can pre-commit to making specific donations and lock them in at the start of the year. Such "commitment devices," as behavioral economists call them, also help change our behavior in other areas, like going to the gym or increasing retirement savings.[74]

While these strategies may seem mechanical, they can help fortify our will to change our ways and ultimately our heart. This is the intentional, thoughtful, and difficult work of becoming generous, and it takes more than empathy. It also takes compassion. We need both. In his essay, "The

Perils of Empathy," Paul Bloom recognizes the value of empathy—to feel what someone else is feeling—as a basic part of intimacy. But when it comes to guiding our moral judgments, empathy makes us "biased, tribal and often cruel." We feel empathy for people we like or who are one of us or who have treated us fairly in the past but show hostility to a competitor. We feel empathy for an "identifiable victim," but shut it down if we believe someone is responsible for their own suffering.[75]

Bloom cites the neuroscientists Tania Singer and Olga Klimecki who distinguish empathy from compassion: "In contrast to empathy, compassion does not mean sharing the suffering of the other: rather, it is characterized by feelings of warmth, concern and care for the other, as well as a strong motivation to improve the other's well-being. Compassion is feeling for and not feeling with the other."[76] In another series of studies measuring emotional empathy and compassion, Bloom found that compassion predicts charitable donations, but empathy does not. While empathy often wears people out, "compassion training by contrast leads to better feeling on the part of the mediator and kinder behavior toward others."[77]

Our generosity increases as we grow in *both* empathy and compassion. Sharing in the suffering of others helps generate empathy. But generosity grows as we practice compassion. The Barna Group found that our meter for generosity goes up the more we give.[78] We need to grow in the discipline of giving. I have stated that giving is a byproduct of generosity. But it's also true that the more we give the more generous we become. This paradox is evident in the tug of war between our intent and our action, between our selfish and our pure motives.

In their book *The Paradox of Generosity*, Christian Smith and Hilary Davidson argue that we reap generosity's rewards only when we don't fake generosity in order to achieve some other, more valued, self-serving end. Fake generosity generates "practices that are not really generous, but rather self-serving—and self-serving actions do not enhance anyone's well-being." For generosity to be authentic, they say "it must actually be believed and practiced as a real part of one's life." That authenticity leads to purity in our giving. However, Smith and Davidson go on to say that we do not need to become completely pure in our motives before we can practice being generous at all. "One of the best ways of starting to become a truly generous person, if one really *wants* to, is simply to first start *behaving* like a generous person. Right attitudes often do follow right actions."[79]

Understanding this paradox of generosity, our organization provides nudges that will prompt donors to give from their hearts. We inject emotion and heart into our campaigns. For example, we might start a campaign, "We know you care about the needs of others. We've seen your previous generosity to the XYZ rescue mission, so today we want to talk to you about an opportunity to extend your generosity." We also encourage donors to look at the deeper motives for giving, what it might do in their hearts and in the lives of the recipients. The question we ask is not,

"What are you giving?" but, "Why do you want to give?"

We then say, "You're building God's kingdom by changing a person's life forever. At the same time, your generosity will change your heart, as you adopt an attitude, a humble posture of giving. And God will reward you in the knowledge that you are helping His kingdom come on earth as it is in heaven."

The Flow of Generosity

Generosity, ultimately, is about love. We are what we love, and our habits both follow and form our hearts. I love giv-

> *Generosity, ultimately, is about love. We are what we love, and our habits both follow and form our hearts.*

ing, and giving continues to transform me. I see that love welling up in little things, like writing checks, instead of using EFT (electronic funds transfer) for my donations. EFT is giving on autopilot. It robs me of the joy of taking my pen, writing that dollar amount twice, and writing out the name of the person I'm supporting. I intentionally release my money to a specific person who will benefit more than I will if I kept that money. The freedom is found in unclenching my fist and grabbing my pen. Generosity is an expression of God's love welling up in my heart. Giving to big philanthropic organizations is great, but I get as much, or even more, joy from giving to one person, like Chris. Generosity doesn't need to be scaled to change the world. In fact, it works most effectively person to person.

Our support for Chris and his brother set them free to begin to enjoy life rather than simply endure their lives. We "primed the pump" to release the flow of generosity into their lives. A similar situation unfolds in the book of 2 Corinthians, when Paul raises a collection for impoverished believers in Jerusalem. Paul encourages the Corinthians to give, and he holds up as an example the church in Macedonia, as I discussed in Chapter 2. He tells the Corinthians, "We want you to know about the grace that God has given the Macedonian churches...their extreme poverty welled up in rich generosity. For I testify that they gave as much as they were able, and even beyond their ability... for the privilege of sharing in this service to the Lord's people" (2 Corinthians 8:1-4). The Macedonians were dirt poor, and yet they participated joyfully in a collection for impoverished believers in Jerusalem. Paul uses the word *charis* to refer to God's gift of grace given to the Macedo-

> *Generosity helps establish God's kingdom of reconciliation and love.*

nians, which enabled their own giving.

The Macedonians demonstrated to the Corinthians that giving flows from being gifted with God's grace. This collection was not a one-off funding campaign for the Jerusalem Christians. It was an expression of *koinania*, a participation and sharing in community, central to Paul's gospel message of giving and receiving (Philippians 4:15), which was at the heart of Paul's gospel message of reconciliation (2 Corinthians 5:18-19). The gospel establishes a new economy characterized by a reconciled humanity who cares for one another. (Some Biblical scholars maintain that Paul's vision was a Christian interior economic system categorized by gift giving between cities.)

Generosity helps establish God's kingdom of reconciliation and love. It transforms the life of the giver as it restores the life of the receiver. It manifests as the fruit of the Spirit growing in our lives. The same love and joy that wells up and flows out of Chris as he gives out of his poverty, also courses through my heart as I number my days, but not my wealth. It is the joy of Jesus who emptied himself of all but love and gave himself over to death to reconcile a lost humanity to God. Hebrews 12:2 tells us that, "For the joy set before him he endured the cross…" What gives joy to the one who made the world and everything in it, and owns that world and heaven, too? What is "the joy set before Jesus?" *We* are his joy. *We* are his reward. When we empty ourselves and give to others as Jesus did, we experience that joy.

But seek first his kingdom and his righteousness, and all these things will be given to you as well.

MATTHEW 6:33

Scripture says for us to seek the Kingdom first. We're to seek things like peace, forgiveness, sacrifice, compassion, kindness, and generosity. God is less concerned about our bank accounts growing and more interested in our hearts growing in kingdom values.

CHAPTER 8

THE POWER TO RELEASE THE WORLD

S ometimes the smallest of moments can open our eyes and change our lives. My friend, Jeudy tells of such a moment. As he sat in a fast food restaurant, he noticed a homeless woman pushing a grocery cart outside. It fell over and her belongings spilled onto the sidewalk. Jeudy saw many people pass her by, but no one stopped to help her, and in that moment this woman became more than a curiosity to Jeudy.

His eyes were opened to her need, and then, beyond, to the needs of the poor and the homeless in LA's urban ghetto where he grew up. It was a world that Jeudy had left behind; he was on track to financial and professional success in the world of marketing. But he couldn't ignore what he had just seen. People simply walked past this woman as if she weren't there. Jeudy started to volunteer with inner city ministries, and as he got more involved, he realized that he needed to follow his heart and dedicate his life to the people that no one saw. He walked away from his marketing career to reenter his old world fully. At the age of 27, he moved into Watts, a low-income neighborhood in Los Angeles[80] known for its high crime rate, as a volunteer. He had no job, no prospects, and no income.

I have known Jeudy for more than 12 years, ever since he was a college student. I have proudly watched him parlay his talent and drive into a successful career. Leaving that behind was a bold, even foolhardy, move—an abandonment of the plans for his career we had discussed together. But I admired Jeudy's courage. And I couldn't deny his heart. I had to acknowledge that Jeudy was demonstrating true generosity—his response to receiving God's amazing love. When we experience God's love, we release generosity into the world.

God opened Jeudy's eyes to the need, and he was now aligned with how God felt about his old neighborhood. He loved it. Jeudy had followed a carefully-set plan to leave the inner city and prosper, and now God was calling him to go back home with no plan and no resources. It seemed crazy, but as Francis Chan reminds us, God's love is outrageous, you could even say crazy.[81] In time I began to realize that God was unleashing Jeudy himself. While God uses all our resources to extend his goodness to the world, it's not what we have, but who we are, that is the ultimate resource. We love as God first loved us. This is generosity.

As I noted in Chapter 3 and elsewhere in this book, generosity is not just about money; it includes how we use our time and even encompasses our general outlook towards others. Once Jeudy's eyes were opened, his heart followed and then his entire life was transformed. To give of himself meant that he needed to move his family into the inner-city neighborhood. He and his wife, Shea, and their 15-month-old son now live in one of the worst neighbor-

When we experience God's love, we release generosity into the world.

hoods of LA—Compton—and Shea is hoping to transfer and get a teaching job there, too.

In this chapter, I want to discuss what happens when God's resources are released to the world through us, which Jeudy's story beautifully demonstrates. Jeudy sent me a blog post he'd recently written which evokes that initial moment that changed the trajectory of his life, the woman and the fallen shopping cart. In his recent post, he tells the story of awaking one morning to the sound of "clinking and clanging." He opened the blinds to see three homeless men searching for cans in the apartment dumpster. Jeudy quickly dressed and ran out to hand them the bags of cans and bottles that he had gathered for this very purpose. He recognized two of the men. One remembered him from a previous encounter and hugged him.

"It was pretty darn cool to know two of them by name," Jeudy wrote, "and to hug Eric...not because I was doing 'outreach,' but because I authentically care for him, and love him as God loves him." Jeudy concludes his blog post,

"May something in your life alarm you…even as I woke up to the clinking and clanging alarm of God's loved people."

Presence

Generosity is unleashed when we open our eyes to see people others ignore, our ears to hear the garbage gleaners, and our hearts to love them and know their names as God does. It's being present even as God is present to us through Jesus. When this theology of presence is put into practice, it will change our lives and our communities.

God is the greatest giver the world has ever known. He gave us the world and everything in it. And then he gave us the gift of his presence, which we can only experience through the gift of his son. These gifts upon gifts pile up so

Generosity is unleashed when we open our eyes to see people others ignore, our ears to hear the garbage gleaners, and our hearts to love them and know their names as God does.

that Paul is overwhelmed and can only exult in 2 Corinthians 9:15, "Thanks be to God for his indescribable gift." Jesus gave everything, died with nothing, and gained the whole world. Jesus was the ultimate giver who established a revolutionary movement that would change all of human history. Borrowing from the terminology of Adam Grant, the psychologist I quoted in the previous chapter, "When givers succeed it spreads and cascades."[82]

Biblical scholar John Walton prioritizes presence as the primary theme that progresses through the Bible:

> The plot line of presence is more important than the plot line of salvation (salvation history). Jesus did not just become human so that he could die for us; he became human to establish God's presence among us as one of us—so we can learn more about how we should live in God's presence.[83]

Walton goes on to say that because God is present to us through Jesus, he has established a partnership with us to accomplish his plan and purpose for the world. In other words, God gives himself to us so that he can *be with* us. And the gift of God's presence spreads out through us to encompass the world and all its people.

Mentorship

It wasn't enough for Jeudy to give money to the homeless. He had to live with them, as God lives with us. Giving spreads and cascades through presence. It's person to person. Many years ago, I went to Cabo San Lucas, and as anyone who has traveled there knows, you can't escape the tiresome timeshare spiel from some eager sales agent. I was accosted by an aggressive agent, and rather than brush him off, I decided to engage him in conversation.

"How much do you make off one of these deals?" I asked him.

"Fifty dollars," he said.

"Tell you what..." I began, but he cut me off with the offer of two free dinners and an additional offer of two free hang-gliding sessions.

"I don't want either of those," I said.

"How about two free dinners, and I'll join you?" he persisted.

I agreed. "As long as you take me to some hole-in-the-wall, off-the-beaten- tourist-path spot. I want local, even if it's bad. I don't care."

"Meet me at the sales booth when I'm back in two days," he said.

Two days later, we both showed up. He took me to an obscure restaurant down a little alley—hot, noisy, and filled with locals. We started to talk, and a few minutes into the

One expression of generosity that I value most is mentoring because it enables me to pour my life into someone else.

conversation he said, "Mr. Randy, I like you. You're different."

"How so?" I asked.

"You actually care." He went on to tell me that no one had ever asked for his story. "But you did," he said.

We talked for two hours about his life, his goals, faith, and family before we said goodbye. The next year I got a Christmas email from him. And four years after that another email from Mexico City. "I'm graduating with a degree in photography," he wrote, "and it's because of you. You told me to go for it."

"Actually caring" sums up my understanding of generosity, and it has guided my approach to helping people over the years. What we give is what a person most needs (and it might not be money); it might also change the course of their lives.

Sometimes giving a person what they need most happens in a one-off dinner meeting in a hole-in-the wall restaurant in Mexico, but it often takes years of involvement with a person. One expression of generosity that I value most is mentoring because it enables me to pour my life into someone else. They can extend what I have taught them into their sphere of influence and into the next generation. It's also a good way to leverage oneself through the life of another. To the extent that I influence that person, I live through them. It's the opposite of living vicariously. We are familiar with the old saying, "Give a man a fish, and you feed him for a day. Teach a man to fish, and you feed him for a lifetime." But we rarely stop to consider the role of the teacher or mentor.

When I first met Jeudy 12 years ago, he was hightailing it out of the Cambodian church that I attended. I followed him out into the parking lot and bribed him with a lunch offer to come back the following week. At lunch, he peppered me with questions which he continued to ask me for the next 12 years. I saw Jeudy baptized, become an outreach leader, lead a missions' team to Ensenada, and develop a homeless ministry on his home turf. When his marketing career took off, we continued to meet every Saturday for Bible study. When Jeudy told me he was quitting his job and moving into Watts I realized that my mentorship did not mean emulation. Jeudy took my advice, but then careened away from it when he followed his heart. This was his way of living generously, a way that put him in a state of complete dependency on God. Jeudy renounced the life he had in order to seek God's kingdom first. And as Matthew 6:33 promises, "all these things" were given to him as well. As he was running out of his savings and ready to cash in his 401K, for example, he was hired as the director of a non-profit in Compton. God met his need.

Mentorship expands our generosity. What we give to others, they amplify and pass on. I learned from Jeudy that generosity can begin not only when we give of our resources, but also when we give up our lives. When we learn to live within ourselves, but also *beyond* ourselves.

Mentoring has become a way of life for me. It's something I do as a matter of course with anyone who spends any amount of time with me. In my last book, I told the story of Danny whose father died tragically when Danny was in the 9th grade with three younger siblings. I gathered Danny, his mom, and his brothers and told the boys I would take each of them on an airplane trip when they graduated from high school. All of them got a one-day trip to San Francisco with me where we rode the rails, trolley, and subway, and visited Alcatraz. It was more than a fun excursion or a new experience. I wanted to sneak into their lives, give them a little odyssey, and be their guide. Mentoring is an art that requires all the qualities that generosity inspires within me: time, energy, intentionality, and compassion. Above all it requires a desire to affect change in someone's life, change that will ripple out into the world.

Capacity Building

Jesus had a growth strategy, which started with him leaving. "And surely I am with you always, to the very end of the age," he says to his disciples (Matthew 28:20). It's yet another strange paradox of a life characterized by paradox.

Mentoring is an art that requires all the qualities that generosity inspires within me: time, energy, intentionality, and compassion.

Jesus not only gave his life *for* his disciples; he gave it *to* them, so that he would be *in* them. And he could only do so by leaving them. Jesus mentored a core group of twelve disciples who, ignited by the Holy Spirit, started a revolution of love that reoriented the whole world to God's gift of grace.

I have tried to pattern my life after Christ's example and by Christ's presence within me, so that others *don't* need me. Compelled by God's work of love in my heart and prompted by God's Spirit, I have poured myself into people. They, like Jeudy, will overflow generosity into a multitude of lives long after I'm gone.

This is why I focused not on growing my money but using it to help people grow and thrive. I call this capacity building. I don't want simply to sustain ongoing projects, but also to identify and help build new ones that are structured for growth. I recently directed my foundation to give a $10,000 grant to a charity in Compton, along with a pep talk to its director: "I know what you do. I like what you do. But I don't want to give to what you do. I want to give to something that will allow you to do more of what you do."

The central paradox of generosity is in keeping with the paradox of being a disciple of Jesus. He who loses (or gives) his life for my sake will find it. He who gives his money away will watch it grow. I understand the verb "grow" to be a transitive verb; money grows something other than itself. When invested in stocks, bonds, or mutual funds, money grows itself. When invested in people, money grows them. In this sense, I don't give money away. I give it to generate growth in its recipients.

Michael Oh, Global Executive Director and CEO of the Lausanne Movement—a global movement that mobilizes evangelical leaders to collaborate for world evangelization—gave a powerful speech at a missions conference a few years ago. His words underscore the fact that it's God's will that we give generously of ourselves and our financial resources. Of this kind of release, he said,

> …money, like blood, was meant to flow. To flow through the body. To cleanse and bless and enrich and support and give life. This is God's design for the money that he has blessed you with. You have opportunity for double blessing, to receive and to give. And

what a shame it is to miss out on the fullness of God's blessing and giving sacrificially and generously for the flow of the blessing for the whole body of Christ... When we believe God's promises in the gospel, we invest generously in gospel purposes. When we don't believe in God's promises, we spend selfishly or hoard fearfully. When we believe we have received a glorious eternal inheritance, we release the ambition to build an earthly inheritance.[84]

Last year, Brewer Direct, the agency I founded, raised $50 million for 40 rescue missions, most of them in smaller cities throughout the United States. We help raise funds for missions whose sole purpose is to restore people through

I don't give money away. I give it to generate growth in its recipients.

feeding, housing, counseling, and medical treatment. They help those who have lost their dignity to reclaim it—and hope to start living again.

In the parable of the sower in Luke 8, the sower scatters the seed that falls on four types of soil. The good soil yields a hundred-fold harvest. This parable has many applications, and here's my takeaway: A harvest requires good seed and good soil. Seed is meant to be sown, to be used up, not stockpiled. Once planted, it needs to be watered until it germinates and grows into a good crop.

Like the seed in the parable, the seed of generosity is sown indiscriminately. Generosity is not selective. It simply flows out from a grateful heart. However, generosity planted in receptive hearts yields a harvest of blessing far greater than the initial gift. John 12:24 reads, "Very truly I tell you, unless a kernel of wheat falls to the ground and

> *Wherever there is disorder and dysfunction of any kind, goodness needs to be restored.*

dies, it remains only a single seed. But if it dies, it produces many seeds." As he prepares to die, Jesus drives his parable deeper into the soil of his disciples' minds and hearts. The grain of wheat expresses the life that comes out of death and counsels releasing one's life rather than fearfully grasping to it. My manifesto for the Randy W. Brewer Foundation reflects this principle: to give until there is nothing left to give. This is my growth philosophy: not to amass more but to give away everything so that God multiplies it in the lives of others. So, as Michael Oh said in his speech it can be released to "cleanse and bless and enrich and support and give life."[85]

Releasing Goodness into the World

Unclenching your fist is a gesture of surrender. Opening your hand wide is a gesture of release. Giving opens our hands and triggers a dual release. First, it releases us from the power that our money exercises over us; second it releases the power of generosity into the world. As I have stated repeatedly in this book, the gospel reorients us to our treasure because it changes our hearts. When God's love invades our hearts, we no longer treasure our money; we treasure people, both rich and poor. When we love rich people, we don't feel inferior to them. When we love poor people, we don't condescend to them. We respect them and expect to learn from them. If money still has power over us, we can give but still look down our noses on poor people. When money no longer has power over us, we can detach ourselves from our money and attach ourselves to people. This is why I will crisscross the world to visit the children whose lives I've invested in. This transcends giving. It's about becoming generous. Matthew 6:22 reads, "The eye is the lamp of the body. If your eyes are healthy, your whole body will be full of light." In some translations the word "good" appears, rather than "healthy." The word good has a double meaning in Greek; it also means generous. A good eye is a generous eye that continually looks for opportunities to give.[86]

A generous eye also looks for ways to release goodness into the world, a goodness that typifies God's creative work, and summarized by God's emphatic declaration at creation: "It is good." John Walton defines goodness as a condition in which something is functioning optimally as it was designed to do in an ordered system.[87] It is working the way God intended. Wherever there is disorder and dysfunction of any kind, goodness needs to be restored. When we do good, we participate in the goodness that

God is producing. And in doing so, we share in God's joy over his creation.

Contrast this to the rich young ruler in Luke 18 who becomes sad when Jesus tells him to give away everything he owns, "because he was extremely rich." His attachment to his wealth and his inability to release it made him sad. The irony of the story is that this young man, having kept all the commandments, was very good, but turned away from the source of goodness, God himself. He mistook being good with enjoying and participating in the goodness of God for the world. He didn't understand that God had provided him with all the gifts that Jesus was asking him to return to God by releasing them to the poor. The ultimate regifting.

God has made generosity part of the structure of the universe. The universe operates by a principle of charity, of God who so loved the world that he gave. When we are generous, we act in the way he himself acts. Once we have received God's gift, we become most like him when we give. And we help restore the world to its original goodness.

When I give, I don't have the whole world in mind. That's God's job. Generosity has enlarged my heart but contracts into intense joy when I focus my giving on one person at a time. Goodness is not abstract. It's specific, granular, and personal. Doing what's good presumes we understand the situation, the people involved, and how to best help them. And it draws out their own goodness, as much as it demonstrates ours.

As I end this chapter, I close my eyes and see Jeudy

hugging the man who was picking through his garbage. I know Jeudy well enough to know that his hug is not only telling his friend that he is loved, but also that he is good. To see that someone is good and to show it is a creative act. When we let others see themselves in the mirror of our generosity, they grow in goodness and extend themselves to others.

But even if I am being poured out like a drink offering ... I am glad and rejoice with all of you.

PHILIPPIANS 2:17

The notion of dying old, broke, and exhausted is about being emptied of everything—for the gain of Christ. My sense is that the one emotion that will stick with me until I am in the presence of Christ is the feeling of not doing enough.

CHAPTER 9

OLD, BROKE, AND EXHAUSTED

H ow much do you need to feel comfortable?"

It was one of the first questions the financial advisor asked when we began working together many years ago. The question is endemic to financial planning. And then, specifically, he asked, "How much do you feel you need to have in your checking account?"

"Let's say $2,500," I said.

"Okay, we'll invest the rest."

Time went on, and a few years later after my business stabilized after the start-up years, the advisor asked again: "How much do you need to feel comfortable?"

This time, the number was much higher, multiple times higher. I said I needed more in my checking account to feel comfortable. And then a few years later, he asked me again. This time, the number was more than six figures. Times had changed, and so too had my level of comfort.

Comfort is a strange emotion. The question about financial comfort is unanswerable, of course, because what is "enough" is always a moving target. Several years ago, we met again. This time, I had recently been diagnosed with throat cancer. When the financial advisor asked the same question again, I replied, "None. Zero. It doesn't matter."

"What do you mean?"

"I don't want to invest anymore," I said. "I don't want to put any more money away. When can I start pulling it out?"

"And why's that?" he said.

"I can't take it with me," I said. "I want to give it away."

So much of the narrative around retirement is about collecting all the possessions and experiences that we've been denied before because of work. The common retirement model is that we work and work and work—and then we retire. Finally, in retirement, we have both resources and an unencumbered, extended time to live life to its fullest. Consequently, the story that financial advisors harp on us until we retire is that we don't have enough. Almost every ad for retirement taps into our "not enough" fear. It's packaged surreptitiously in the form of sandy beaches in the spring, lakeside living in the summer, apple orchards in the fall, and ski slopes in the winter.

That's not to say that I don't value saving for retirement, getting out of debt, and becoming good stewards of what God has entrusted to us. I certainly valued the help from this financial advisor. But, on that day, I asked him to stop investing my money. Cancer has a way of recreating reality. Our most scarce resource is rarely money; it's time. Often we don't fully grasp that essential truth until it's too late.

Desire of the Heart

In 1989, I was 30 years old and working for a fundraising agency. I don't remember exactly what motivated me to do so, but I wrote this on a sheet of paper and pinned it to the wallboard in my office: "I will retire on August 28, 2011."

"And what will you do then?" a colleague asked.

"Travel," I replied. "I will travel the world and give to charity."

At 30, I didn't know exactly what I was saying, of course, but I did know that I wanted to combine my love for travel

Cancer has a way of recreating reality. Our most scarce resource is rarely money; it's time. Often we don't fully grasp that essential truth until it's too late.

with my passion for giving. I was in the business of helping raise money for other organizations, and I saw firsthand the impact of generosity. My timing was off by a few years, but today, I am living out my vision from 1989. It's not exactly like I had planned, of course. I didn't foresee two bouts of cancer. And I also didn't fully anticipate building a business that I would sell, freeing me to accomplish my goal.

Early on, though, I made some choices that put me on the path to retire early so I could travel and give. The first was to get out of debt. The second was the decision not to marry. Later came the opportunity to start a business. Today, with the exception of what I need for the end of my life, living as I do with cancer, I would just as soon not have *any* money. With no family, my needs are simple. I've put together three goals for my remaining years: to die old, broke, and exhausted. ("OBE," for short.) I have little control over my first goal—dying old. I'm currently fighting another form of a cancer as I've mentioned in previous chapters, and only God knows my future. Isaiah 50:57 says, "Because the Sovereign LORD helps me, I will not be disgraced. Therefore have I set my face like flint, and I know I will not be put to shame." I, too, have set my face like flint, asking the Lord to grant me the desires of my

> *Because of the relationships that I've nurtured the past ten years, I have a legacy that will extend into the next generation.*

heart. I'd love to live into my eighties, being tired from seeing the world and exhausted from helping people—and to be out of money. To have lived without regret.

A few of us can still remember "The Partridge Family," the TV comedy that aired in the early 1970s. The show starred Shirley Jones as a widow who took her five kids on the road as a pop band in a tricked-out school bus. David Cassidy played Keith Partridge, the oldest son who played guitar and made the teenage girls swoon. A few years ago, David Cassidy died at age 67, and his daughter Katie Cassidy posted this on Twitter: "My father's last words were 'So much wasted time.'"[88]

Just recently, after learning of my cancer, a young person

whom I've mentored asked, "Any major regrets?"

"Nothing major," I said. "If I have any regret, it's that I didn't deal with some of my family drama early on in adulthood so that I could have resolved those issues." I wrote about some of our family's struggle to love and show love in my previous book, *Finding My Voice*. Not until right before the death of my parents was I able to address some of my pain from growing up in a family where even the simple acts of love, grace, and concern for one another were scarce.

"Do you have any regret that you didn't get married and have kids?"

"I have kids everywhere," I said. And I do. My legacy is not biological children who will pass on the Brewer name in future generations. The business I started could change its name from Brewer Direct to another. All that is food for worms. But because of the relationships that I've nurtured the past ten years, I have a legacy that will extend into the next generation. At this juncture of life, as I said in Chapter 4, I want whatever time I have left, as Paul said in Philippians 2:17, to be "poured out like a drink offering..." I don't want my last words to be ones of regret. I don't want to leave this earth with unreleased time and stored-up resources.

On recent trips to both African countries and Indonesia, my hosts have fretted about my health. "Randy, you need to rest more," they said. I really don't need more rest. What I need in this moment is fewer meetings, and I've taken steps to strip back my schedule to only that which is most essential. I need to be in Africa and Southeast Asia.

I need to be able to look into the faces of those I love and listen to their hopes for a better future.

Just recently I was on the phone with a young man with whom I call every three months. We met some years ago on one of my overseas trips. He is not someone of faith… yet. Right before we closed the conversation, he asked, "Given your prognosis, what matters to you right now?"

"Relationships," I said. "Everything else burns."

In the last scene of *Schindler's List*, the movie about the man who risked his life to save 1,200 Jews during the Holocaust, Oskar Schindler reflects on his heroism with no small measure of regret.

"I could have got more out," he says. "I could have got more. I don't know. If I'd just…I could have got more."

"Oskar, there are eleven hundred people who are alive because of you," says Itzhak Stern, Schindler's accountant who assisted him with the rescue of Jews.

"Look at them."

"If I'd made more money…I threw away so much money. You have no idea. If I'd just…"

The dialogue goes back and forth, with Schindler finally saying: "I could have gotten one more person… and I didn't! And I … I didn't!"[89]

That is the regret of someone who is on the front lines, who, in pouring out his life, sees not what he has done but instead what's unfinished or left undone. I, in no way, can understand how Schindler felt nor do I compare my own generosity with his wartime heroism to save Jewish lives. However, I have felt that pain of regret earlier in my life.

I had developed a friendship, for example, with a young professional in Thailand. I shared Christ with him and sent him materials about faith and Christianity. His work brought him to the US once, and he even visited church with me, though he never made a personal commitment to Christ, that I know of.

Later, back in Thailand he contracted meningitis, but I had no idea how serious it was. One day I received a couple voicemails from him and because he lived in a different time zone, I didn't have the chance to call him right back. I listened to his voicemails, and he seemed fairly articulate: "Randy, I'm gonna get better. I'm gonna get stronger again. Thank you for your prayers."

The next day I got a call from a mutual friend, Dan, who also lives in Thailand. He told me that my friend was gone. Apparently, he woke from a coma, left me a series of voicemail messages, and then died. He had been in a community hospital because of his low income. Meningitis is often deadly, no matter where you live, but I felt like I could have done more. I had access to resources near where he lived in Asia. "If I'd known, I could have …"

"Randy, you know, you have no idea how you changed his life," said Dan. "He was so unhappy and miserable ever since his sister had died very young of throat cancer, but since he talked to you and visited you there, he was so positive and happy, I can't explain it."

I appreciated Dan's words, but it was cold comfort.

The notion of dying old, broke, and exhausted is about being emptied of everything—for the gain of Christ. My sense is that the one emotion that will stick with me until I am in the presence of Christ is the feeling of not doing enough. Some may say I am a bit narcissistic to think that my efforts can make a dent in the suffering of the world. But pushing myself to do as much as I possibly can creates in me the energy and focus to keep working. In earlier chapters, I made the point that generosity involves loss. As you give away, you lose resources—time, money, and even energy. But ultimately what we gain is far more than what we lose. As we empty ourselves, as I discuss in Chapter 7, we are actually in a position to receive—to be filled up with so much more: joy, relationships, and contentment.

The Emptied Life

The exhausted part of "old, broke, and exhausted" is not a cliché or some sort of heroic, feverish aspiration of youth, a redux of the first half of life. Pouring out one's life is really first of all a mindset, a way of looking at the world as Christ sees it. It begins with the basic Christian understanding that preserving your life is the surest way to lose your life. And for many, including me, you really can't fully grasp the notion of losing your life to save it until you are faced with your own mortality.

Jesus demonstrated the ultimate act of emptying by becoming a man and suffering death—and a painful one at that. The theological word for emptying is the Greek word "*kenosis*"—it's the idea of Christ voluntarily "emptying" his own will by becoming a human. It's his complete and utter receptiveness to the will of God: "… rather, he made himself nothing by taking the very nature of a servant, being made in human likeness" (Philippians 2:7). As I've endured both the physical and psychological effects of cancer, I've come to appreciate Jesus' agony in the Garden of Gethsemane. This side of Jesus is not often discussed—his human anxiety at the ultimate emptying of his life and what was about to transpire:

He took Peter and the two sons of Zebedee along with

> *Pouring out one's life is really first of all a mindset, a way of looking at the world as Christ sees it.*

him, and he began to be sorrowful and troubled. Then he said to them, "My soul is overwhelmed with sorrow to the point of death. Stay here and keep watch with me." Going a little farther, he fell with his face to the ground and prayed, "My Father, if it is possible, may this cup be taken from me. Yet not as I will, but as you will" (Matthew 26:37-39).

This is one of the most dramatic exchanges between Jesus and his Father in the New Testament. It is raw, unfiltered. It reveals the internal distress at the real threat of death. While my diagnosis doesn't alter my core beliefs, it has rattled me at times. When you stub your toe, your toe hurts. You grab your toe, hold it, and utter: "Ahhh!" You let yourself feel the pain. It permeates your whole body, and you feel the throbbing for a few moments. But then it subsides. You realize that it's just a momentary toe stubbing. I have felt the throbbing, those dark and angry moments of distress. I have started to spiral downward with *Why me? This is just unfair.* I think, *I'm finally at this place where I can do the work for which I've been called.* I find consolation in Jesus' inner torment at Gethsemane. It's important to note that, after his disciples fell asleep, Jesus prayed a second time. This time the wording is slightly different: "My Father, if it is not possible for this cup to be taken away unless I drink it, may your will be done" (Matthew 26:42). In that hour timeframe, Jesus had understood, I believe, the final answer. It was God's will for him to die. That knowledge, however, did not obviate his anguish on the cross when he cried out, "*Eli, Eli, lema sabachthani?*" which means, "*My God, my God, why have you forsaken me?*" (Matthew 27:45).

I too pray, "If there's any other way, let this cup pass

> *Releasing generosity, even with all its benefits, is not merely about freeing yourself from bondage. It's ultimately about freeing others still in bondage.*

from me." When I'm at my most positive, I think, *King Hezekiah, in Second Kings, was on his deathbed, and he got fifteen more years.* The prophet Isaiah had come to the king and said, basically, "You're a dead man." Scripture says, "This is what the Lord says: Put your house in order, because you are going to die; you will not recover" (2 Kings 20:1). Hezekiah reminds the Lord of his faithfulness. This short sentence is breathtakingly powerful: "And Hezekiah wept bitterly." It pretty much sums up the honest emotion of someone receiving a death sentence. As Isaiah is making his way out of the court, Isaiah receives a word from God: He has heard the prayer of Hezekiah and promises him fifteen more years of life.

I have many days when I pray like Hezekiah, "God, give me mercy. Give me 15 more years." But then I look at my life the last seven years since my bout with throat cancer and think, *Maybe God has already given me seven more years.* The places I have experienced, the work that I have done, the people I've met—God may have already answered my prayer. And maybe God will give me seven more years. I don't know. But I am free. I truly want to be old, broke, and exhausted. I want to end well, feeling content that I poured out my life until the very end of my days.

Free at Last

If I had a single message to the younger generation it would be this: stop collecting and amassing and hoarding stuff. And get out of debt. Debt is the antithesis of freedom. Debt is bondage. And when you're trapped in bondage, you are not able to release what you've been given to others. Others, then, continue to suffer as a result.

Releasing generosity, even with all its benefits, is not merely about freeing yourself from bondage. It's ultimately about freeing others still in bondage. Your bondage stands in the way of the freedom of others. You have a purpose. You have work to do. To be free means the chance to free others. That's the releasing. That's living.

One day at a time, find a way to be free. And start today. Everything in this life, all the stuff, will burn. None of what you think matters today will travel with you once you cross the great river Jordan into eternal life. Nor will any of it matter when you are on the shores of the Jordan, late in life, waiting to cross. Even if you are able to retire early for several decades of travel and grandchildren and long weekends at the family cottage—you don't want to live mostly for self. To receive God's richest blessings, you must empty yourself. While you are still young, be free with your time, your talent, and your treasure. Be free with your stuff. Be free in your heart. Be free with your love, your compassion, and your grace. In your freedom, you will free others. It's an internal detachment from the stuff of this world that will release your generosity to others. All generosity begins and ends in the heart. It's always a loosening, a bringing, a maximizing, a leveraging, an inspiring—all words synonymous with *releasing* what's been given to you.

Releasing generosity is available to anyone at any point in their life.

The last job my father had was in his late 70s and early 80s. He served as a hospitality coordinator for a local savings and loan. The financial institution had a corporate lunchroom which was used by the business and nonprofit community for lunch meetings and other events. The idea, of course, was to imprint the brand of the bank on its community with more time in the bank itself. My father scheduled the events, coordinated the food, and after the event was over, he cleaned up. My father immediately took notice of the leftovers—often quite a bit of food—still fresh or packaged for future use.

One day, he loaded up the remaining food which included sandwiches, bags of chips, salads, and cookies and other desserts into the trunk of his car. He then drove to the town where I was raised—a low-income, industrial community—and dropped off the leftovers at an auto-mechanic shop where he had serviced his car in years past. The garage was owned by several Hispanic brothers, and almost every day, around 3 PM, my father would pull up, open the trunk, and lay out the goods. The other mechanics in the shop, neighbors, gardeners, as well as my father gathered round, kibitzed, ate, and shared their lives.

My father's simple act of redistributing the leftovers released generosity into this out-of-the-way, forgotten neighborhood. He could have simply tossed out the food and gone home to watch TV. But his simple act of generosity released the joy of food and conversation into a community of day laborers. At 84, my father passed away, and the folks from the mechanic shop attended his funeral, paying their final respects and thanking our family for his generosity.

As I reflect on my life, I return, always, to the quarter that my father gave me when I was six years old. Something passed between my father and me when I reached for the quarter: It was a set of values about releasing what's been given to me. I now pass that on to you. May you take the "quarter" that has been given to you and release it into the world, so that the Father can bless others.

ENDNOTES

Chapter 1 | **Life with No Outlet**

1   Charities Aid Foundation, www.cafonline.org/ (February 2, 2016).

2   Christian Smith, Hilary Davidson, *The Paradox of Generosity: Giving We Receive, Grasping We Lose,* (New York: Oxford University Press, 2014), 103.

3   Ibid.

4   Christian Smith, Michael O. Emerson, Patricia Snell, *Passing the Plate: Why American Christians Don't Give Away More Money,* (New York: Oxford University Press, 2008), 29.

5   Jonathan Meer, David H. Miller, Elisa Wulfsberg, "The Great Recession and Charitable Giving," National Bureau of Economic Research, http://www.nber.org/papers/w22902/ (December 2016).

6   Elie Wiesel was quoted in an interview with Alvin P. Sanoff, *US News & World Report,* October 27, 1986.

7   Kerry Hennon, "I'm Rich, and That Makes Me Anxious," *The New York Times,* https://www.nytimes.com/2017/11/07/your-money/wealth-anxiety-money.html/ (November 7, 2017).

8   Paul K. Piff et. al, "Having Less, Giving More: The Influence of Social Class on Prosocial Behavior," *Journal of Personality and Social Psychology,* Vol. 99; no. 5, 2010, 779-781.

9   CareerBuilder, "Living Paycheck to Paycheck is a Way of Life for Majority of U.S. Workers, According to New CareerBuilder Survey," http://press.careerbuilder.com/2017-08-24-Living-Paycheck-to-Paycheck-is-a-Way-of-Life-for-Majority-of-U-S-Workers-According-to-New-CareerBuilder-Survey/(August 24, 2017).

10 Bob Sullivan, "State of Credit: 2017," Experian, https://www.experian.com/blogs/ask-experian/state-of-credit/(October 24, 2018).

11 Laurie Rivetto, "More Money, More Problems?", Michigan State University, https://www.canr.msu.edu/news/more_money_more_problems/ (May 16, 2017).

12 Meera Jagannathan, "The More Money You Make, the More Stressed You Get," Market Watch: https://www.marketwatch.com/story/the-more-money-you-make-the-more-stressed-you-get-a-new-study-says-2018-04-17-9883523/ (April 17, 2018).

13 Raj Raghunathan, "Why Rich People Aren't as Happy as They Could Be," *Harvard Business Review*, https://hbr.org/2016/06/why-rich-people-arent-as-happy-as-they-could-be/ (June 8, 2016).

14 Ibid.

15 Paul K. Piff et. al, "Higher Social Class Predicts Increased Unethical Behavior," *Proceedings of the National Academy of Sciences*, http://statmodeling.stat.columbia.edu/wp-content/uploads/2016/06/Piff-et-al-2012-PNAS.pdf/ (March 13, 2012).

16 Jerry Useem, "Power Causes Brain Damage," *The Atlantic*, www.theatlantic.com/magazine/archive/2017/07/power-causes-brain-damage/528711/ (July/August 2017).

Chapter 2 | **The Generosity Machine**

17 The research for the Hebrew words for generosity came in the form of an interview and exchange of emails with Dr. Steven D. Mathewson, author of *The Art of Preaching Old Testament Narrative and Risen: 50 Reasons Why the Resurrection Changed Everything*.

18 Timothy Keller, *Generous Justice: How God's Grace Makes Us Just*, (New York: Viking, 2010), 15.

19 Ibid.

20 Dan Olson, "The Time Is Ripe for Radical Generosity," The Gospel Coalition, https://www.thegospelcoalition.org/article/the-time-is-ripe-for-radical-generosity/ (Dec. 26, 2014).

21 Craig L. Blomberg, *Christians in an Age of Wealth: A Biblical Theology of Stewardship*, (Grand Rapids, MI: Zondervan, 2013), 96.

22 Ibid., 100.

23 Scott J. Hafemann, *The NIV Application Commentary: 2 Corinthians*, (Grand Rapids, MI: Zondervan, 2000), 330.

24 Ibid.

25 Ibid., 334.

26 Christian Smith, Hilary Davidson, *The Paradox of Generosity: Giving We Receive, Grasping We Lose*, (New York: Oxford University Press, 2014), 12.

27 Ibid., 177.

28 Ibid.

29 Craig L. Blomberg, *Neither Poverty Nor Riches: A Biblical Theology of Material Possessions*, (Westmont, IL: InterVarsity Press, 1999), 196.

Chapter 3 | **Enlarging the Heart**

30 Blaise Pascal, *Pensées VII*, 425.

31 Dacher Keltner, "The Compassionate Instinct," *Greater Good*, https://greater good.berkeley.edu/article/item/the_compassionate_instinct/ (March 1, 2004).

32 Daniel Goldman, "Why Aren't We More Compassionate?", TED Talk, https://www.ted.com/talks/daniel_goleman_on_compassion/ (2007).

33 Francis Chan, Crazy Love: Overwhelmed by a Relentless God, (Colorado Springs, CO: David C. Cook, 2013), 69.

34 Philip Yancey, *Finding God in Unexpected Places*, (Colorado Springs, CO: WaterBrook, 2005), 195.

35 This quote is referenced on the website Catholic.org (https://www.catholic.org/clife/teresa/quotes.php).

36 Alexandra Larkin, "167 People Paid It Forward at a McDonald's on Father's Day," CNN, https://www.cnn.com/2017/06/20/us/indiana-mcdonalds-pay-it-forward-trnd/index.html (June 20, 2017).

Chapter 4 | **Releasing Financial Benefits**

37 Kate Bowler, "Death, the Prosperity Gospel and Me," *The New York Times*, https://www.nytimes.com/2016/02/14/opinion/sunday/death-the-prosperity-gospel-and-me.html (February 13, 2016).

38 Kate Bowler, *Everything Happens for a Reason: And Other Lies I've Loved*, (New York: Random House, 2018), 21.

39 Elizabeth Dunn et. al, "Spending Money on Others Promotes Happiness," *Science*, Vol. 319, Issue 5870, 2008, 1687-1688.

40 Zoë Chance and Michael Norton, "I Give Therefore I Have: Charitable Donations and Subjective Wealth," *Advances in Consumer Research*, Vol. 38, 2012, 150-151.

41 Ibid., 150.

42 Entrepreneur staff, "Giving Makes You Rich: New Proof that it Pays to be Charitable," https://www.entrepreneur.com/article/185662 (October 17, 2007).

43 Ibid.

Chapter 5 | **Releasing Psychological Benefits**

44 Rick Warren told the story of his wife learning about the orphan crisis in an interview on belief.net in 2005. (https://www.beliefnet.com/faiths/christianity/2005/10/rick-warrens-second-reformation.aspx?p=3#DxHJEg I6yXS4HYcC.99).

45 Kay Warren's Orphan Care Initiative can be found at http://kaywarren.com/orphancare/.

46 Soyoung Q. Park et. al, "A Neural Link Between Generosity and Happiness," *Nature Communications*, Vol. 8, Article number: 15964 (2017).

47 Gretchen Reynolds, "Giving Proof," Well, The New York Times Magazine, https://www.nytimes.com/2017/09/14/magazine/giving-proof.html (September 14, 2017).

48 Soyoung Q. Park et. al, "A Neural Link Between Generosity and Happiness," *Nature Communications*, Vol. 8, Article number: 15964 (2017).

49 C.S. Lewis, *The Weight of Glory*, (San Francisco: HarperOne, 2001), 46.

50 University of British Columbia, "Thinking About God Leads to Generosity, Study Suggests," *ScienceDaily*, (www.sciencedaily.com/releases/2007/08/070829102048.htm).

51 Francesca Borgonovi, "Doing Well by Doing Good. The Relationship between Formal Volunteering and Self-reported Health and Happiness," *Social Science and Medicine, Vol. 66, 2008*, 2321-2334.

52 Christian Smith, Hilary Davidson, *The Paradox of Generosity: Giving We Receive, Grasping We Lose*, (New York: Oxford University Press, 2014), 17.

Chapter 6 | **Releasing Physical Benefits**

53 Sara Konrath, "The Power of Philanthropy and Volunteering," *Wellbeing: A Complete Reference Guide*, Vol. 6, (Malden, MA: Wiley Press, 2013), 410.

54 Ibid., 413.

55 Ibid., 410.

56 Ibid., 410-413.

57 World Health Organization, "Fact Sheet: CVDs," https://www.who.int/news-room/fact-sheets/detail/cardiovascular-diseases-(cvds), (May 17, 2017).

58 American Heart Association, "Stress and Heart Health," https://www.heart.org/en/healthy-living/healthy-lifestyle/stress-management/stress-and-heart-health, (June 2014).

59 Mayo Clinic Staff, "Chronic Stress Puts Your Health at Risk," https://www.mayoclinic.org/healthy-lifestyle/stress-management/in-depth/stress/art-20046037, (March 19, 2019).

60 WebMD Staff, "Stress Symptoms," https://www.webmd.com/balance/stress-management/stress-symptoms-effects_of-stress-on-the-body#1, (July 11, 2017).

61 Rodlescia S. Sneed and Sheldon A. Cohen, "Prospective Study of Volunteerism and Hypertension Risk in Older Adults," *Psychology and Aging*, Vol. 28(2), June 2013, 578-586.

62 Thomas Merton, *Seasons of Celebration*, (New York: Macmillan, 2010), 103.

63 Thich Nhat Hanh Foundation, "Practice of Generosity," https://thichnhathanh foundation.org/practice-of-generosity.

Chapter 7 | **Generosity's Great Mystery**

64 As quoted in Mark Twain on *Common Sense: Timeless Advice and Words of Wisdom from America's Most-Revered Humorist*, (New York: Skyhorse Publishing, Inc., 2014), 19.

65 Rene Girard, *The One by Whom Scandal Comes: Studies in Violence, Mimesis, & Culture*, (Michigan State University Press, 2014), 17.

66 Evangelical Council for Financial Accountability, "The Generosity Project," 2017, 11.

67 World Population Review, http://worldpopulationreview.com/countries/ kenya-population/, (2019).

68 Mary Grace Costa, "Five Facts about Mexican Slums," https://borgenproject. org/about-mexican-slums/, (April 4, 2017).

69 Adam Grant, *Give and Take: A Revolutionary Approach to Success* (New York: Penguin Books, 2013), 4.

70 Ibid., 10.

71 Ibid.

72 BBC News, "Why India's Rich Don't Give their Money Away," https://www.bbc. com/news/world-asia-india-47566542 (April 2, 2019).

73 Timothy Keller, *The Prodigal God* (New York: Penguin Group, 2008), 60-62.

74 Raymond Fisman and Michael Luca, "How to Suppress Your Inner Scrooge" *The Wall Street Journal*, https://www.wsj.com/articles/how-to-suppress-your-inner-scrooge-1512746205, (December 8, 2017).

75 Paul Bloom, "The Perils of Empathy," The Wall Street Journal, https://www.wsj. com/articles/the-perils-of-empathy-1480689513, (December 2, 2016).

76 Ibid.

77 Ibid.

78 Barna Group, "What Motivates Christians to Give?", https://www.barna.com/ research/motivations-for-generosity/, (November 27, 2018).

79 Christian Smith, Hilary Davidson, *The Paradox of Generosity: Giving We Receive, Grasping We Lose*, (New York: Oxford University Press, 2014), 7.

Chapter 8 | **The Power to Release the World**

80 *The Los Angeles Times* offers a more complete description of the Watts neighborhood at http://maps.latimes.com/neighborhoods/neighborhood/watts/.

81 Francis Chan, *Crazy Love: Overwhelmed by a Relentless God*, (Colorado Springs, CO: David C. Cook, 2013), 65.

82 Adam Grant, *Give and Take: A Revolutionary Approach to Success* (New York: Penguin Books, 2013), 10.

83 John H. Walton, *Old Testament Theology for Christians: From Ancient Context to Enduring Belief*, (Downers Grove, IL: InterVarsity Press, 2017), 28.

84 Michael Oh, "The Individual's Suffering and the Salvation of the World," a speech given at The Gospel Coalition's 2013 Missions Conference, https://www.youtube.com/watch?v=45wpuMLSiLg (April 7, 2013).

85 Ibid.

86 Craig S. Keener, *The IVP Bible Background Commentary: New Testament*, (Downers Grove, IL: InterVarsity Press, 2014), 63.

87 John H. Walton, *The Lost World of Adam and Eve: Genesis 2-3* and *The Human Origins Debate*,(Downers Grove, IL: InterVarsity Press, 2015), 59.

Chapter 9 | **Old, Broke, and Exhausted**

88 Andrea Mandell, "Katie Cassidy shares father David Cassidy's last words: 'So much wasted time,'" USA Today, https://www.usatoday.com/story/life/people/2017/11/24/katie-cassidy-shares-father-david-cassidys-last-words-so-much-wasted-time/893367001/ (November 24, 2017).

89 The full script of *Schindler's List* by Steven Zaillian can be found at https://www.imsdb.com/scripts/Schindler%27s-List.html.

CHAPTER 1

LIFE WITH NO OUTLET

1. What are some ways you've experienced the "inlet" of God's love—or generosity—in your own life?

2. How has God's biggest gift—the sacrifice of his Son—created an "outlet" of love in your life?

3. Read Mark 12:41-44. The widow "put in everything—all she had to live on" (Mark 12:42). Why was the widow in this verse willing to give so freely? What does this demonstrate about the connection between faith and giving?

4. In contrast, why did the wealthier people refrain from generosity?

5. With whom do you identify, and why?

6. If the love of money is the root of all evil, how should we frame our relationship with money?

7. How might you slow down to recognize the needs of those with whom you come in contact?

8. What is one simple act of generosity that you can perform today?

CHAPTER 2
THE GENEROSITY MANDATE

1. What is the relationship between righteousness and generosity?

2. Is generosity a direct commandment from God? If so, what examples of generosity do we see in the Old Testament?

3. Read 2 Corinthians 8:1-5. What conclusions can you draw about the Macedonians and why they gave so liberally? Why do you think the Macedonians considered it a "privilege" to be generous?

4. How does generosity have an impact on our spiritual formation? If we aren't generous, what does that reveal about our faith in God?

5. If all we have—including our talents, personalities and experiences—are gifts directly from God, why aren't we more generous with others?

6. We are commanded to take care of others, but often look the other way. What simple behavior can you change today to engage those with less than you?

7. How do we "right the world" when we are generous? Can you share an example from your own life?

CHAPTER 3
ENLARGING THE HEART

1. Read Matthew 9:35-38. What moved Jesus to compassion? How did he demonstrate compassion? From these verses, how would you define compassion?

2. From your experience, would you agree that most people have a "compassionate instinct"? Why?

3. How have you experienced compassion in your life? From others? From God?

4. What inhibits compassion? Is if fear of not having enough? Or is it simply not caring for or thinking about the needs of others?

5. What simple step can you take to begin caring for your neighbor or person with whom you work?

6. How is compassion related to generosity?

7. Christian author Randy Alcorn has said that if you have a heart for something, you should invest in it. What do you have a heart for, and how are you investing in it?

CHAPTER 4
RELEASING FINANCIAL BENEFITS

1. Read Luke 6:38. What is the promise of this chapter? How might people misuse this scripture? Is there danger in giving with the expectation of receiving in return?

2. Why is it so easy to fall into the trap of believing that greater success, or greater wealth, equals more happiness?

3. Do you agree that you reap more financially when you are generous? Why?

4. How can we go against the grain of the Prosperity Gospel when it comes to the definition of success?

5. When hard times hit, how do you frame God's generosity? How does the Bible frame it?

6. Name various ways that God has blessed your life. Why do we tend to take these blessings for granted?

7. How is God's economy different than the world's? Where do you see God's economy at work in your life?

8. How does the act of giving bring God's kingdom to earth?

9. What might we receive through our generosity?

10. How can you seek the kingdom of God first in the everyday?

CHAPTER 5
RELEASING PSYCHOLOGICAL BENEFITS

1. When you think of "God's image," what characteristics come to mind?

2. How do Christians reflect God's image to the world?

3. Describe a time that you experienced joy because of being generous? Where do you think that joy came from?

4. The science indicates that we are made to be generous. We "light up." It makes us feel better. If this is true, why aren't we generous all of the time?

5. Read 2 Corinthians 9:6-7. What does cheerfulness have to do with giving? What happens when we give cheerfully rather than reluctantly or "under compulsion"?

6. What might you be missing out on by not "cheerfully" giving?

CHAPTER 6
RELEASING PHYSICAL BENEFITS

1. Read 1 Timothy 6:17-19. What does it mean that when we practice generosity, we "take hold of life that is truly life?" How might this relate to our overall well-being? What life are we missing out on when we don't practice generosity?

2. Do you buy the idea that our physical health increases as we are more generous? Why or why not?

3. One study cited in this chapter points out that when you are generous, you are more likely to be in community. And people in community are healthier. Have you seen this in your life or another's life?

4. How do you grow stronger through generosity?

5. If generosity is one antidote to stress, how might you deal with a stressful day this week?

6. Practicing generosity that leads to overall health is a discipline. What new and simple discipline can you start implementing today?

7. How do you reconcile the big idea of this chapter with the basic fact that many generous people get sick?

CHAPTER 7
GENEROSITY'S GREAT MYSTERY

1. Would you agree generosity is a "great mystery"? Why or why not?

2. Re-read 2 Corinthians 1-4. With the Macedonians as our model, what should motivate us to give?

3. What are common motivations for giving?

4. What personally has motivated you to be generous in the past?

5. What's the danger of giving with the expectation of receiving?

6. What do you see as the key differences in generosity among different generations?

7. If you're a parent, grandparent, or mentor, how can you help the next generation more fully understand generosity?

8. What are your thoughts on "being intentional" about giving? How can you be both intentional and led by the Spirit?

9. Randy writes, "Generosity doesn't need to be scaled to change the world. In fact, it works most effectively person to person." Do you agree with this? Why or why not?

10. How are we personally transformed as our generosity transforms the lives of others?

CHAPTER 8
THE POWER TO RELEASE THE WORLD

1. Read Matthew 6:33-35. What does "seeking first" the kingdom of God look like? What do you think the gifts are that you will receive in return? Why is this way of living revolutionary?

2. How was Jesus a revolutionary in terms of generosity?

3. Describe a person you know who is a revolutionary in acts of generosity.

4. Randy argues that as you partner with God in generosity you experience his presence more fully in your life. How do you think we experience God's presence?

5. When generosity is planted in our hearts, it yields a rich harvest of generosity. How can we prepare the "soil" of our hearts?

6. Describe a time when you saw God multiply generosity. What, in your opinion, stops the multiplication?

7. Why is it we can be "very good" Christians, like the young ruler, but give ourselves a pass on being generous?

8. This week, how will you let your generosity "flow like blood"?

CHAPTER 9
OLD, BROKE, AND EXHAUSTED

1. Read Philippians 2:1-11. Why did Christ pour out himself as a drink offering? What happens to us when we empty ourselves? Why is emptying ourselves so difficult to do?

2. If you died today, what would your regrets be? Would not being generous be at the top of the list?

3. What do you want to be remembered for? What do you want your legacy to be?

4. Once people hit their latter forties, they start to worry more about retirement: "Will we have enough?" Or, "Will I have enough?" If you knew for sure that you would have "enough," how would that change your giving behavior?

5. What does Jesus' prayer in Garden of Gethsemane show us about his humanity?

6. What is the correlation between "dying to self" and "freedom"?

7. What does a life of "emptying" look like for you? What one thing do you need to give up to discover God's freedom for your life?

8. If you knew the time you had left on earth was limited, how would you want to spend the last months or years of your life?

9. How can you make the most out of the years you have left on earth?

Made in the USA
Columbia, SC
13 February 2020

87891583R00100